HELP YOUR
CHILD LEARN
HOW TO LEARN

HELP YOUR CHILD LEARN HOW TO LEARN

Marie L. Avery and Alice Higgins

PRENTICE-HALL, INC.
Englewood Cliffs, New Jersey

Help Your Child Learn How To Learn

© 1962 by Marie L. Avery and Alice Higgins

Library of Congress Catalog Card Number: 62-17775

Printed in the United States of America

38669-T

This volume is dedicated to
the children from whom we have learned
the things that help them to learn

ACKNOWLEDGMENTS

In presenting for the first time this complete "program for learning," we would like to pay tribute to some of the many people who have aided us in its development.

We particularly thank:

Westridge School, Pasadena, for the opportunity to work with the staff and the students

the teachers of All Saints School, Archdiocese of Los Angeles, especially Sr. M. Macrina O.P., Principal, Sr. M. Vivian O.P., Sr. M. Clarus O.P. and Anastacia Cassidy

Ethel Sheldon, former head of Sequoyah School and Frances Pryor, Reading Co-ordinator, La Canada Public Schools, for their co-operation, interest and encouragement

Dr. Leon Oetinger, San Marino, and Dr. Milton Tobias, Beverly Hills, for the knowledge and assurance we have gained from their research

the teachers and parents who have tested some of our ideas and who have passed on to us many of theirs

Dave Hall for his sensitive art which illustrates our program to the student with clarity and simplicity

and, above all, Rex Barley and Edward R. Grade, who sifted and co-ordinated the mass of material from which this book was constructed, for their invaluable editorial knowledge and assistance.

CONTENTS

INTRODUCTION

The "Why" of This Book

As they stand on the threshold of the coming age and watch the unfolding wonders of the new technology, today's parents must ask themselves what they can do to prepare their children for the demands of that age. No haphazard exposure to knowledge will equip a child to compete in a world of increasing automation, in a society where the number of college graduates will be greater than ever before.

Already there has been an increase in the demands made on the student in every school grade. The pressure is coming not only from parents, teachers, school administrators, and school boards, but from the diverse needs of our times as expressed by the heads of government and industry.

Recognition of the existence of this challenge should not be left until the parent hears those discouraging words from the teacher, "Your child is not keeping up," or "Your child needs help at home."

There is no doubt that you, as parents, want the best education available for your children. Americans have been raised with complete faith that their heritage of an education for all will not be denied them. Teachers and school administrators hold the same conviction, and they are struggling to meet the requirements of vast enrollments, changing methods, and constant criticism. There seems to be no letup in sight, and America has the task of reassuring its young citizens that their vital educational heritage is intact.

Can this be done? Yes—with the cooperation of parents in making the teachers' work more fruitful. This calls for an energetic acceptance of the fact that the ability to learn is a skill that can be acquired and developed, and that this process is best begun during the period of mental awakening.

No definite period in a young child's life can be tagged the best time to begin training. Basic learning is a very gradual process, and the psychological moment for specific steps varies among children and can even vary in time sequence in an individual child. One thing is definite, however: If certain basic concepts are established before a child starts kindergarten, he will be much more successful throughout his school years and, in consequence, throughout his whole life.

Parents, including those who have had no preparation as teachers, can give the training at the "psychological moment" and at any other time a child shows he needs it.

The purpose of this book is to describe in logical sequence the principles and concepts necessary to learning and to give suggestions for activities that will help to perfect the inherent skills of any child.

If this training has been undertaken at home, the teacher is free to teach all the material that is required in each grade. Even if a child does not do well after he has started in school, the parent can still help by picking up some of the steps that may have been neglected. The teaching plan that follows has been developed through years of observing the patterns used by educators across the country to aid the process of learning.

It was a prime concern of our forefathers that every individual should have the opportunity to reach his true destiny and fulfill his obligation to himself and society. To this end, they sought to make a good education available to all.

A good education is the goal of this teaching program, and we present it now in the conviction that your concern is no less than that of our forefathers.

HELP YOUR
CHILD LEARN
HOW TO LEARN

PART I

PERCEPTION TRAINING

Chapter 1

THE SENSES

For many years it has been known that the main channels used for receiving messages from the outside world are the five special or exterior sense organs and their connections with the brain. Those channels receive impressions through all stimuli that can be seen through the eyes, heard through the ears, felt through the skin, smelled through the nose, and tasted through the mouth. The impressions enter each channel separately and individually, but if they go into the brain together, their future association is assured. It is also true that if the senses are used simultaneously, the messages themselves are cabled so that perception and recall are strengthened and thus the learning process is aided.

There are other senses, known as *interior* or *organic*. These may be considered under the classification of *feeling*. Specifically, *feeling* implies the use of touch, but it can also encompass sensations that arise from stimuli originating in the organs or in variously located physical areas. Hunger is "felt" in the stomach, thirst in the throat; fatigue, pain, temperature, pressure, and movement are felt throughout the body. Recognition of time and rhythm is felt in the muscles and joints, and the conception of space has an indefinite locale.

To a baby, the tactile or touch sense is basic. Through the sense of touch in his lips, a child learns his first lesson more easily than he could through his eyes, ears, nose, or taste organs. Later, he becomes aware of feelings that are pleasant or unpleasant. He is made comfortable or uncomfortable, and he reacts accordingly. Inner senses inform him of hunger, thirst, pain, movement, balance, pressure, and fatigue, and his exterior senses eventually allow him to perceive the causes of these sensations.

Each of the feeling areas has its own degree of intensity and its own reason for existing. Hunger and thirst are eliminated by the food and drink needed for life. Pain, which has various causes, is the warning of something wrong. Awareness of temperature and the extremes of heat and cold are felt in a specific part of the brain and to a child is but a sense of comfort or discomfort until he is old enough to associate cause with effect. Pressure is eventually associated with weight, which can be heavy or light or moderate.

But none of these sensations has a meaning in the communications sense until a child's vocabulary has been built by hearing words, using his voice to reproduce the words, and associating the words with what he feels.

For example, when precisely can a child tell what is meant by the word *cold?* He must first experience a certain sensation caused by contact with ice, cold water, or cold air. He must realize how these stimuli produce reactions in his body. Only then can he associate the reactions with the word *cold*. He will also have to recognize how that feeling differs from one produced by *heat* or any other stimuli.

Perhaps more attention should be given to the fact that some children actually do not make the associations needed for a clear knowledge of sense reactions—that they require training in perceptions that, to experienced adults, have become second nature. A child may appear to be lacking in intelligence when all he needs is perception training in a big world that to him is filled with new and complex concepts.

Another interior sense is that of position. A baby, or any individual for that matter, needs to know where he *is* in his own egocentric world. Only from there can he find his way around in the world about him. He is in the center; around him are left and right, up and down, back and front. Each individual has a feeling of dominance toward either the right or the left. Ordinarily, this feeling is toward the right, as is indicated by the way our world has been arranged to accommodate right-handed people. For that reason, being left-handed is sometimes inconvenient, but as far as learning is concerned, it is no more serious than that.

If the eyes, ears, hands, or feet have unlike dominance, there may be some confusion in the brain, where the various stimuli responses meet. Because of this, training in recognition of the objective meaning of left and right is very important. The activities given in this book for that purpose can be very helpful in the event that some areas of dominance are crossed.

Orientation in the location of up, down, back, and front is also an important part of the learning process. The concept of direction, combined with distance, involves measurements and any concept concerning placement of symbols or objects in a given space. Pressure, force, energy, movement, speed, rhythm, and sequence are other concepts that must be perceived if learning is to be complete.

Perception of these concepts by the interior senses is trained by using the exterior sense organs to work with objects. Perceived from an egocentric point of view, the recognition of many concepts is one thing; the recognition of the same concepts from the standpoint of objects outside oneself is another. Relationships become relative, and the child must be given opportunities to practice with a variety of objects in many ways—to sort, compare, and analyze them.

To some children, perception may seem to come easily, but some, including many very bright children, are held back because they need one perception channel or another opened more fully. There are many keys that can be used to unlock the gates that may be holding back a flood of greater understanding.

The five exterior sensory channels receive stimuli from the outside world. The more of these senses that are stimulated at the same time, the stronger is the response. Touch requires direct contact with an object. Hearing requires contact between the ear and sound waves—vibrations that spread out in ever-increasing size from the source of the sound. Distance can be estimated by sound. Irregular vibrations affect pitch, speed, and pressure. Seeing requires no contact—merely the medium of light and the object within the line of vision. The sense of smell is stimulated by gases and vapors coming from objects or substances. Smells may be pleasant or unpleasant, sweet, sour, or spicy; their association with objects or events makes perception more complete. Taste, sometimes hard to distinguish from smell, is stimulated by contact of the taste organs, mainly on the tongue, with chemicals; it can also produce feelings of hot or cold. Taste, like smell, contributes to full knowledge of many things seen, heard, or felt. When all the senses are employed, total perception results.

A child who has never perceived an apple, can see and feel it is round and perhaps smaller than his ball. He sees its color, feels its smoothness and hardness, and estimates its weight. He smells it and, if he eats it, knows that it tastes sweet or sour. Possibly it is cold. He experiences pleasure or dislike, and he may realize that it satisfies his hunger or makes him less thirsty. He hears the noise it makes when his teeth bite into it. Someone may say to him, "That is an apple." Thus, all the outer sense channels are stimulated, as well as several of the inner senses. They all contribute to his knowledge of an apple and what makes the object an apple, not an orange, not a doll, not a baseball. He has grasped the *abstract* idea of apple.

Similar processes of perception take place in the acquisition of everything the child learns. Sometimes learning is accomplished by association, by noticing likes and differences, by comparison. But for total perception, no possible step should be neglected. If there are any gaps in the child's development, they must be filled in.

Patterned, sequential learning, started early in a child's life, precludes the possibility of such gaps occurring. Consider the amount of information a child gathers in one year by testing over and over again the impressions received through the senses of seeing, hearing, smelling, touching, and tasting, in conjunction with his inner senses. The facts are amazing. Concurrently, he also is establishing patterns for recognition. Nowhere does the word *recognition* have better application. Analyzing it from its Latin origins, *re* means *again, cognitio* means *a getting to know*. Over and over again, a child gets to know something through one channel, then through another, until it becomes a part of his very life.

To illustrate this phenomenon, imagine a staff of five trusty messengers bringing you important news dispatches. The decision you are about to make depends directly on what these messengers tell you. One messenger comes in with a report, which is made as accurately as his ability permits. The second messenger is ready and waiting to confirm, deny, add to, or modify the first dispatch. The third, fourth, and fifth act in the same way. When one message has been distilled from the five, it is stronger than any of its individual parts; stronger, in fact, than the sum of its parts, because of the necessary selection of the intersecting and unifying elements. It has become one strong, meshed cable of many strands. Nature has provided for this cabling of senses, and it behooves us to make the utmost use of any untapped resources of the human brain.

What, then, does this mean as far as your child is concerned? It means that each sensory channel must be in the best possible working condition. It means that each channel should be ready for use in association with every other channel until, at last, all messages through every channel are cabled, thereby reinforcing and adding strength to the learning process.

How can each channel be trained to operate efficiently by itself or in conjunction with others? When should all the senses be trained?

The answer to both these questions is the same: Follow a pattern of perception training that includes the use of all the senses when the child is ready, no matter how early in life. Impatience for the right moment to appear may cause a feeling of frustration, but by watching carefully you will find that even a baby can begin to associate sounds and touch or any other of the sense combinations very early.

After messages or stimuli have been perceived and recognized, the child faces the task of classifying and sorting them. One often sees a baby look at his hand from amusing angles, then nibble at it to reassure himself that it is really his. Suddenly he loses interest and seems to conclude, "Yes, it's mine. It looks right and I can feel it."

You cannot follow his thought processes and tell precisely how he has sorted it all out and made his calm but world-shaking decision. If during the rest of his early years he were allowed to inspect things from every angle and study them through as many senses as possible, his perception might be just as easy, his recognition and classification of information just as obvious and correct.

His hand is not abstract. It is an object, there for him to examine and re-examine in whatever ways his still unchanneled senses can accept. Even more fundamentally, he will reach out for stimuli while showing no interest in abstractions such as pictures and symbols representing what he knows. At last, he will seem to be satiated with feeling, seeing, and hearing the things in his immediate environment. He knows them. Perhaps his ability to sort and classify them has reached its peak. This, then, is the time to present new fields to conquer.

A vitally important step in the sequence of learning is the *recall* of things perceived, recognized, and sorted. Another is the appropriate *use* of information gathered. Unless it can be recalled, everything has been in vain; and, as a corollary, unless it is recalled and returned through the sorting, recognizing, and perception processes, it cannot be used in any way to communicate ideas to others.

This may sound like a complicated, frustrating pathway. It can be, of course, but with a careful survey of what faltering steps each child must go through, plus an understanding of what the child faces with each new situation, it falls into place and becomes quite simple. In fact, it becomes just plain common sense.

The methods involved in seeking and selecting information are important. There must be movement and energy in each step. There must be movement within each organ as well as in the process of attaining information. After the individual's brain has made the initial move and the sensory channel has been ordered to bring in the message, a complicated but definite chain of action is set in motion within the brain. Here is the point at which you, whose concepts have long since been established, can first help your child in the long process of learning.

It is not enough just to perceive; one must perceive correctly. Later, speed can be added to accuracy.

No one would try to give perception-training activities to a tiny baby. However, his environment can be prepared in such a way that he is given the opportunity to find his own pattern. Just as he, by nature, learns to creep before he walks, he should handle fundamental shapes of objects before he learns their specific attributes and uses. If he has blocks and spheres to play with, he will pick them up, feel them, examine them and throw them away. He will prepare himself for more advanced practice in actual perception training.

Just as perception training proceeds from handling three-dimensional objects to working with two-dimensional forms, then to learning the use of symbols to represent abstract ideas in various forms of communication, so does the entire learning process follow a sequential pattern. Even though much material taught in schools may not follow the sequential patterns shown in this book, it seems logical to suppose that it is advantageous for a student to see the fundamental sequential order on which subjects are based.

A child may learn to read and learn to read well before he knows the names of the letters. Nevertheless, there is a way in which reading can be broken down to show its sequential pattern. A child can go back and fill in any gaps that may have been left in his learning process. He can learn the names of the letters, how to make them, their sound patterns, and the way they are put together to make words. He can learn how the words are put together in grammatical patterns to make sentences, and how sentences put together in proper sequence make paragraphs. Finally, he will see how the paragraphs are used to give him all the information used in every subject he studies.

History, obviously, started at the beginning of known time and proceeded in sequence to the present. Yet the subject of history, as well as geography, arts, sciences, and literature, is usually taught from the standpoint of immediate environment—first studying the things closest to the child, then spreading out to those far away or long ago. However, it is sometimes more helpful to better understanding to let the child see the complete picture on a time-line basis. Similarly, numbers had a beginning in time, and a pattern such as that presented in this book sometimes promotes a better understanding of number concepts and processes.

No attempt is made to replace methods already used. What is shown here merely supplements what has been learned and helps to give the child a clearer understanding.

Chapter 2

CREATE A CLIMATE
FOR LEARNING

Prerequisites for good learning are good physical and emotional conditions. If there is confusion around your child, he himself is likely to be confused. You may feel that you cannot always control situations, but if a disturbance exists, you should seek advice from qualified sources or make a special effort to reorganize your own life—or at least protect your child from its influences.

If your child has physical disorders, there are doctors and clinics to help him. If the child has neurological disturbances, pediatricians can be consulted about medication. Also, you should realize that perception training often alleviates some of these problems.

With those contingencies recognized, faced, and cared for, freedom from hunger and pain are usually enough to keep a baby happy. This alone creates his confidence in you, the parents or adult who is caring for him.

You should foster this feeling of confidence by treating the child as a human being, helping him to retain his dignity, and stressing his good points. You should not laugh or make fun of him when he is serious. He does not always understand that laughter sometimes indicates approval.

Your experience and training give you the right to expect obedience from your child. You should be able to choose the areas in which your superior knowledge enables you to fill a position of command. If you have this certainty within yourself, you can in turn appeal to his sense of what is right. When you give an order that you know is justified, you should follow it through and make sure that it is obeyed. If this is not done, future orders will certainly be ignored.

You should not hesitate to admit an occasional mistake. Then show the child how mistakes can be acknowledged, forgiven, and made right. This re-establishes confidence in adults—a confidence that might well be lost if too many mistakes are made and disregarded.

You should not make a promise that you cannot keep. If unforeseen circumstances necessitate a change of plans, an explanation is due the child. It is good to have schedules set up, but they can be subject to necessary changes.

You should give your child enough attention so that he never feels the need to demand more. Overstimulation is one of the greatest blocks to learning; it can be brought about by too little or too much attention. Common sense should be your guide here. You should not force your child to change from one interest to another too quickly or too often. Too many interests contribute to confusion and overstimulation. So many things around a child are new to him that he needs time to examine and perceive them. As he grows older, he can gradually take more and more. You should be sure that your child has neither too few nor too many interests. You can usually tell by his attitudes whether one or the other condition exists.

Help your child to learn to accept responsibility by first giving him tasks to perform which he can accomplish easily; the complexity of the tasks can be increased as ability increases. The important thing is to make him realize that there are some things that he needs to do. He must come to recognize that he, and he alone, is responsible for his own actions, even though you as his parent have the right to judge his performance. Praise him when he proves his dependability.

You should give your child some individual attention every day. Even though there may be several children in the family, a little time can be taken out of a busy day to let each one know that he is important as an individual. Some event that seems trivial to you may be a major event in his life. Let him tell you about it. As he grows older, this may lead to the sharing of joys, fears, and problems that will insure greater family understanding.

The best way to use this book is to go through all the activities with your child, regardless of his age or ability. The perception-training activities in the early sections are planned for very young children, but they can easily be changed for use with older students. For the more advanced child, the later activities for listening techniques can be reworded. Following directions and giving directions can be made into a game. Any child up to the age of 11 or 12 is likely to enjoy taking part.

The eye-training exercises can definitely be used by students of any age. High school students often become faster readers after this type of exercise. Sometimes their ability in sports increases, particularly in such games as baseball, tennis, and basketball, where they use their eyes to follow a fast-moving ball.

Although older children may not need the repetition given for making and sounding letters, their penmanship, spelling, and recognition of words can be improved by studying the chapters on reading. The exercises on sequence stories will improve comprehension.

If you know what your child is studying in school, in what steps he is weak, and what he does not quite understand, you can tell which part of this book will be most valuable to him.

Children are usually quite shrewd about their own good points and shortcomings. If you go through the sections with one and ask him, "Do you really understand this part?' or "Are you sure you know this step?" the chances are he will be able to tell you himself whether or not he needs further training.

When the time comes to start the training periods, have everything needed at hand. If special materials are required, have them ready before you begin. Sometimes the child will be able to help you to collect and organize the objects you need.

Have everything extraneous cleared away so the child will not be distracted. Try to make him feel happy and excited because you and he are going to do something together—something that is fun as well as important. Help him to feel that what you are going to do will prove that he is a very capable person. If he is a child who needs more confidence in himself, be very sure that he does the things he can do; help him until he can do them easily himself. Make him feel successful.

As soon as the child shows evidence of being tired, stop. Plan to continue later, or another day. If the fatigue seems to be feigned, try to revive interest by suggesting new reasons for continuing the activities. Perhaps he will want to learn something especially well so he can show some other member of the family how cleverly he performs; possibly he will respond to further praise.

Try to keep him eager. Do not force him in a way that will make him dislike the whole thing. Keep the exercises on the level of games or exciting new experiences not necessarily related to school work. Of course, preschool children may like the idea of "playing school," but older children may not. The game angle should be stressed.

Be sure to keep everything in orderly sequence. If the child does any part so well that he does not need the practice, go through it cursorily anyway in order not to break the pattern.

You would do well to read the entire book before you use it. At least, read over carefully the part to be used at one time. Understanding the reasons for each step and familiarizing yourself with the material will do much to insure successful presentation and satisfactory results.

An important part of the learning process is the use by the child of a vocabulary that builds as his perception increases. You will find in the appendix to this book a series of vocabulary charts; it is strongly recommended that you study these word lists before you proceed with the daily lessons and endeavor to incorporate as many of them as possible in the activity sessions. Encourage your child to understand and use more and more of these basic words as his comprehension increases and as he progresses to higher grades.

Chapter 3

INTRODUCTION TO PERCEPTION

Your first goal must be to encourage your child to perceive quickly and accurately in every possible way, but most importantly with eyes, ears, and hands.

To do this requires the understanding of many things. Motion is fundamental to learning. It is a first cause of change in matter and therefore an integral part of the similarities and differences that distinguish one thing from another. All the sense organs are equipped to receive stimuli produced by motion, and in order to respond fully, they must themselves move in some part and to some degree.

A child must move his eyes correctly, smoothly, and easily before he can become visually skillful. For instance, he must move them from left to right and back again for reading and writing. Eye-movement training, given to children early and repeatedly, helps them to read more readily and with more enjoyment. When they are very young, children have the inclination to "do it again." That is the time to train this skill. Repetition without fatigue is tremendously important.

The use of the hands is also involved with motion. The small muscles of the hands must be ready to perform many activities, beginning with kindergarten tasks and continuing through learning to write, draw, and handle manipulative devices.

The readiness of these muscles to perform must be insured. Motion in various parts of the body starts long before the hands are used for specific, regulated activities. A baby exercises his muscles by throwing his arms and legs about. Eventually he reaches for objects. When a baby is hungry, he normally evidences much activity until he is satisfied; then he relaxes.

There is also much body activity when the baby is trying to reach for objects. When he starts to creep, he is preparing for the next step—learning to walk. He is trying to find his way about and is training his senses of orientation. Until he has attained his goal, he keeps moving.

While he is doing any of these things, he must be able to make judgments of direction, distance, and space relationships in order to reach his destination, to touch something, to get where he is going, or merely to keep from bumping into things. His eyes must be trained to synchronize with his movements.

If a child's perceptions and skills are trained in the right order, he is more likely to attain the goals for which he is ready, and consequently, he will be less likely to be overactive.

In the early sections of this book, the activities are planned to train perception sequentially and objectively, at first by using concrete objects of three-dimensional form.

Shape and size can be determined by both touch and sight. Color is the only attribute that must be perceived by the eyes alone. Sound is heard only by the ear, but the vibrations can often be felt. Texture can be perceived by the sense of touch only, although, by association, the noise made when the surface is rubbed gives a clue to its smoothness or roughness. The senses are used in various combinations to perceive qualitative and quantitative impressions.

Recognition of the number of a group of objects is perceived without actually counting as soon as the relation of one or more than one is noticed. Communication by use of abstract symbols or numerals comes later. This objective recognition is fundamental to an understanding of mathematics, so it is an integral though unstressed part of perception training.

Color is a help to learning in that it provides a medium for finding likes and differences, for sorting, and for arranging objects in sequential patterns. Selection of degrees of intensity and judgment of relationships by combining colors provide valuable training. The satisfaction that results from observation of pleasing colors and combinations of colors produces creative ideas and appreciation of beauty.

The differentiation of odors and tastes, with recognition of their specific and distinctive savors, particularly in association with other impressions communicated by the other senses, is a part of total perception.

Perception training does more than sharpen the senses. It establishes a pattern for logical thinking, for living an orderly life, for making moral judgments based on truth.

Ideas, like objects, can be arranged in patterns. Some ideas are of greater importance than others. The elements of one idea can be tested against the elements of another and judged accordingly. The elements of a line of thought or action can be examined from the standpoint of cause on the basis of objective facts, and the process of selection, rejection, and choice can lead to the ultimate result and finally to sane, reasoned judgment.

It is with these basic purposes in mind that the activities that follow have been designed. None of them should be confined solely to use on one day. They should be learned on the first day and after that practiced over and over again, every day, until you are satisfied with the child's progress. Then, and only then, should you go on to the next lesson.

Most of the lessons require no special equipment or devices, but where they are necessary, most homes will be able to provide them without difficulty, or they will be available at nominal cost at any toy or variety store. Everything should be at hand before the lesson is started to avoid running the risk of losing the child's attention while you search for a piece of equipment.

Chapter 4

TEACH YOUR CHILD
HOW TO LEARN

Before anything else can be attempted, your child's ears must be trained to fulfill their purpose. Sound waves may enter his ear so that he hears the sounds, but this is not enough. He must be able to interpret them by listening carefully and understanding what they mean.

Sound can be used to associate, to add to the total perception of objects and ideas. It also has significance in its own right, its own abstract being. Sound plays a significant part in the field of communication through speech and music. In order to be interpreted as symbols of meaning, variations of sound must be recognized.

The force of sound, as evidenced by degrees of loudness, is perceived by the auditory sense and can be felt through the vibrations of the air waves. Irregular vibrations, which affect pitch, speed, and pressure, contribute to the forming of sound patterns used for communication.

Sounds of various kinds strengthen the recognition of number, likes, and differences, as well as sequence.

AIMS

1. To train the child to listen carefully.
2. To help him to distinguish differences in sound, tone, and pitch.
3. To help him to recognize differences in time and rhythm.
4. To teach him to recognize the differences between soft and loud.

PRETEST

1. Can your child listen carefully?
2. Can he distinguish variations in pitch, tell high from low?
3. Can he tell which of two sounds is the closer?
4. Can he "keep time" to music or to counting?
5. Can he tell which of two sounds is louder?

MATERIALS NEEDED

1. A pitch pipe or musical instrument. If neither is available, changes in pitch can be judged by using three glasses containing different amounts of water. Tap the rim of each glass lightly with the handle of a spoon. The one containing the most water makes the highest sound.
2. Two pencils with erasers.
3. Two rubber balls.

Activities   Sound three notes—low, medium, and high. Say something like this: "The first sound you hear is low, the next is medium, the next high. Listen carefully and see if you can notice the difference."

Do this several times, changing the order occasionally to high, medium, low or high, low, medium, or any other sequence. Ask the child to tell you the sequence of sounds, after he has listened to them.

Take a pencil with an eraser and tap the top of the table three times with the eraser end. Say to the child: "Listen carefully. Then you tap the table in the same way with your pencil." Notice if he leaves the same time-space between the taps. Continue until he does it exactly right.

Vary the number of taps and the length of the spaces between and have the child imitate what you do. Vary the rhythm by making irregular patterns. Practice tapping softly, a little louder, and then still louder.

Take a rubber ball and give one to the child. Bounce your ball on the floor once and ask the child to listen; then do the same with his ball. He may need practice in bouncing and catching the ball. If so, have him sit on the floor or bounce the ball on the table so it will be easier to catch.

Increase the number of bounces you ask him to follow. Count the number to yourself so you can check his accuracy. It is not necessary for him to know the numerical symbols for the number of bounces, just the inner feeling of recognition of the number. He can count them aloud later, when he has learned the numbers.

The child must listen carefully, feel the number within his consciousness, recall the sounds, then reproduce them by action. The bouncing routine can be varied by changing speed, time-spacing, and rhythm.

Supplementary Activities   If you can do so effectively, use your voice to demonstrate pitch, time, rhythm, speed, and intensity of sound. Ask the child to respond in the same way with his own voice.

If you can do so, make sounds similar to the soft vowel sounds, such as *a* in apple, *e* in Eskimo, *i* in Indian, *o* in octopus, and *u* in umbrella. Stress the differences in these sounds and how he must use his mouth, lips, tongue, teeth, and breath differently for each one. (The relation of these sounds to the letter sounds need not be mentioned; this is handled in a future lesson.)

Have the child practice whispering, speaking softly, then loudly.

After this series of lessons in the recognition of sounds and rhythm as such has been accomplished, you can proceed to activities aimed at improving his listening powers as they are applied to intelligent absorption of instructions.

Certainly nothing can be accomplished unless your child learns to follow directions and follow them correctly, in sequence, from beginning to end.

AIMS

1.   To hear and understand.
2.   To listen carefully.
3.   To retain and recall.
4.   To follow directions correctly and in sequence.
5.   To use these skills in learning how to learn.

PRETEST

1. Does your child listen when you speak to him?
2. Does he pay attention to what you say?
3. Does he remember what you tell him?
4. Can he follow directions?
5. If you tell him to do a sequence of things, can he remember and do them in the right order?

MATERIALS NEEDED

Nothing but the furnishings of your home.

Activities Say something like this: "When you go to school, the teacher will tell you things to do. Sometimes she'll tell you only one thing at a time and sometimes two things and even three things. You will have to listen and hear how many things to do. You will have to understand and remember which to do first, which to do second, and which to do third.

"Today we're going to start learning to listen and to do. I'll tell you something, just one thing, to do. You listen, then say it back to me, to be sure you hear me right, then you do it.

"1. Listen to hear.

"2. Say it to understand.

"3. Do it.

"Ready?

"Go quickly to the front door."

Nod when he repeats the instructions correctly. When he returns, say: "Good! Now I'll tell you two things to do. Be careful now. Be sure to say it after I do.

"Go slowly to the front door and run back quickly."

Now if your child repeats it correctly, watch carefully for the sequence of going slowly to the door and quickly back, since this includes the reverse of the first instructions. If he has not repeated it correctly, say it again, separating the two activities with emphasis.

"Go slowly to the front door."

Pause.

"Run back quickly."

When he has done this correctly and you have praised him, you can give him a sequence of three things. Say:

"Go to the living room, find the book under the chair (name a particular piece of furniture), hop to me with it in your hand, and I will read you a story."

Be sure to read him the story if he succeeds.

The next step in this line of training is to vary the sequence of instructions. One time, give him three things to do; another time, one; another time, two.

Be careful to keep these sequences simple and clear, but add other steps until he has accomplished the skill of doing several sequences correctly. He must feel that he has succeeded in learning to listen carefully and in following directions correctly.

Chapter 5

LEARNING TO
LOOK AND SEE

If your eyes were stationary rather than movable organs, you would have to move your head to look at everything that was not directly in front of you. However, the eyes are made to move to the right and to the left, up and down, and around.

You may have noticed that some children do move their heads while reading or looking at pictures. If, before starting to read, they had learned how to move their eyes properly, they would have been potentially better readers.

This chapter deals with activities that will train eye movement. Keep the training period short. Watch the eyes and observe their movement; you probably can tell if the action has slowed down. The child himself will tell you when he has had enough.

AIMS

1. To move the eyes smoothly from left to right.
2. To move the eyes up and down.
3. To use the proper eye movements in looking and seeing.
4. To increase visual efficiency.

PRETEST

1. Move a pencil or a finger from left to right before the child's eyes (about 18 inches away). Do his eyes follow it? (Put red polish on the fingernail.)
2. Move the pencil or finger up and down, and check the eye's movement.

3. Move the pencil or finger around in a circle from left to right. Do his eyes follow it? The child may not perform this eye movement smoothly and with a consistent rate of speed, but if the correct training is given, he is bound to improve.

MATERIALS NEEDED

1. Objects around the house.
2. The pictures accompanying this chapter.

Activities Read carefully the things you will say before you start giving directions to the child. Choose two objects, such as two pieces of furniture, ten or twelve feet apart on the same side of the room. Chairs will do if the tops of the backs are at the child's eye level. Stand or sit with the child, about ten feet away from the chairs.

Say something like this:

"When you learn to read, you will do it better if you use your eyes in just the right way. In fact, if you use your eyes in the right way now, you'll see and learn more about everything. If you can use them fast, you'll learn faster, too."

Point to the object at the left.

"Look at the chair. Did you turn your head? Don't move your head; you can move your eyes much more easily than you can move your head. This time, be sure *not* to move your head—just move your eyes."

Point to the object on the right. If he does move his head, just put your hand on the top of his head, lightly, so he feels any movement that it makes. As soon as he is able to move his eyes without moving his head, say: "Good. Now make your eyes move from this side"—point to the object on the left—"to this side"—point to the object on the right.

"Good. Now we'll do it again—first slowly, and then faster."

This activity is best when done two or three times a day, but for short periods.

For another eye-training activity place an object in the center of a table. Have the child move his eyes from this object to a corner of the table, and back, then to the next corner and back, and so on to each corner and back to the center. Two times around is sufficient for the first few sessions; the action can be speeded up as he improves in ability to move his eyes smoothly and quickly.

The printed cats shown here are for eye movement at reading distance. Turn to the strip of cats and place it on a table before the child. Talk about the cats, then say something like this:

"This line of cats can help you learn to use your eyes as you will use them when you start to read. When you read you will start here." Point to the large cat on the left. "Your eyes will go across to the little cat." Point to the little cat. "Don't move your head, just move your eyes. Follow the arrow to the next line. Start with the little cat, and let your eyes follow the cats across to the big one. Come right back to the big cat on the top and go across again. This is the way your eyes move when you read."

Continue this training for a few seconds—about ten times across and back.

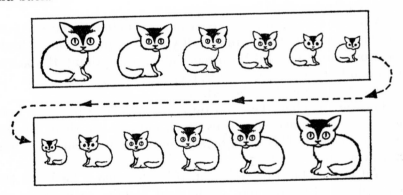

Supplementary Activities If you have a blackboard at home, you can draw pictures of objects (or of any shapes, such as circles or ovals) in sequentially decreasing sizes similar to those of the cats. These may be larger and may be placed at a greater distance from the child. Point to the pictures with a pointer, moving from left to right using a steady, rhythmic motion and a speed geared to individual ability.

The picture of the owls accompanying this chapter is a device for training the eyes to converge, a skill very necessary in reading. A child must be able to look up from a book, then back to find his place. His eyes must refocus each time he does this.

With a slip of paper, cover all but the two owls at the top.

Have the child look at them as you talk about them. Then slide the paper down to the next pair of owls, saying something like this: "These owls are closer together. Move your eyes downward as I slide the paper. These owls are even closer."

Move the paper down again. "Now what? Only one. Let's do it again."

He can move the eyes either up or down with this picture and give invaluable eye training in preparation for the time when the child will read. Be sure to watch for the first sign of fatigue, at which time you should stop.

Summary and Check   Your child should now be able to move his eyes properly. Watch him as he looks at books or draws pictures. When you read to him, let him follow the words with his eyes as you move your finger across the page. Check to see if he is hearing, listening, and following directions.

Color is another integral part of our world. It adds to the depth and breadth of perception. Even to those who are color-blind, color has great importance since the strength of the color rays that are reflected from any object varies and changes the tone or density of color. It is perhaps more important to work on color variations with a child who is color-blind since his choices must come through a much less definite reaction to stimuli, and finer distinctions must be made.

Actually, red, yellow, green, and blue are the only colors that contain no suggestion of another hue, so from the standpoint of sensory perception, they, with black and white, are primary colors. All other hues, as many as one hundred found in the spectrum, are results of mixing. Red, yellow, and blue can be mixed to produce any of the other colors.

For our purpose, six colors—red, orange, yellow, green, blue, and purple or violet—will be used. Red, yellow and blue are usually accepted as primary; orange, green, and purple will be called secondary.

AIMS

1. To give skill in recognizing and identifying colors and their proper sequence.
2. To help the child to recognize similarities and differences of colors.
3. To help him recognize degrees of intensity of color.
4. To help him learn primary and secondary colors.
5. To lead him to an understanding of color in nature.

PRETEST

1. Can your child name and identify the six basic colors?
2. Can he name colors in a proper sequence?
3. Does he understand the process of mixing colors to make other shades and completely new colors?

MATERIALS NEEDED

1. Crayons—red, orange, yellow, green, blue, and purple or violet.
2. A sheet of thin white paper.
3. The figure, showing seven concentric circles, found on page 27.
4. A box of water colors, containing the colors red, yellow, blue (separate pats or refills can be purchased at any art store). Pencils, with colored lead, could be substituted.
5. Two dishes of water and a cloth.
6. Heavy paper for use with the paints.

Activities Place the thin white paper over the picture and trace the concentric circles. (Older children may like to make their own circles, using compasses.) Say: "Use the crayons now. Which is red?" If the child does not know the names of the colors, now is the time to have him associate the names with the colors.

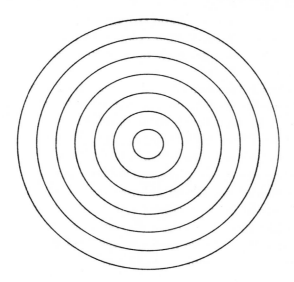

Say something like this: "Color the band farthest from the center with the red crayon." Give him time to color the band; if he does it neatly, it will take some time. To make it a solid color, he would have to press hard on the crayons; shading lightly is easier, but he should make the crayon go back and forth in the same general direction.

Tell him which color to use next, making sure that he associates the name and color. The sequence should be red, orange, yellow, green, blue, and violet.

Continue: "We'll stop with the violet. The small circle in the center we shall leave white. We are lucky. We can't often see a whole round rainbow. If we could, it might look something like this. Sometimes we can see another rainbow on the outside; the colors then are in the opposite sequence. If you like, you may try to make bands on the outside of this round rainbow. See if you can follow the lines around. First, after the red, make a purple or violet band, then blue, green, yellow, orange, and red. These colors on the second rainbow should be a lighter color. Now you have a rainbow within a rainbow." Give the child plenty of time to complete each color band.

Then say something like this: "Now, let's make a rainbow that looks more like the one we usually see, as if it ended on the ground and was made of colored stripes. Close your eyes and think of how a rainbow looks. Which color is on top? That's right, red. Then, what? Yes, orange. Now open your eyes. I'll make a rainbow for you."

Dip the brush into one dish of water; show him how you roll it with a circular motion on the pat of red paint, emphasizing how to get paint on a brush without scrubbing the cake. Make a good-sized arc of red on the paper; then, deliberately, put some red paint in a dish with the brush. Wash off the brush, dry it, then roll it on the yellow, and put some yellow paint in the same dish, mixing the two colors. If you do this slowly and dramatically, the mental picture of your procedure will remain with the child. Say something like this: "See, the color becomes orange when I mix the red and yellow. We've made orange, and that is the color we need for the next stripe of the rainbow."

Paint the next stripe quickly, and say: "Now close your eyes again, and try to remember the next color. Good, it is yellow. How did you know? You remembered, but you also knew that orange comes between red and yellow; that's the way it is in a real rainbow. The sunlight goes through the moisture in the air and light is reflected. The rays are bent and reflect different colors. The ray that makes red is bent the least."

While talking, paint in the yellow stripe, wash the brush, and be ready to mix yellow and blue to make green.

Say something like this: "Close your eyes and tell me which color comes next. That's right, green. Open your eyes. Green must be an in-between color like orange, because we have only red, yellow, and blue paints. They are the primary colors. You know what *primary* means; it means first. These are the colors we start with. We mixed red and yellow to make orange. The last stripe was yellow. What can we mix with yellow to make green, if it's an in-between color? Blue, of course."

Mix the yellow and blue paint and make the green arc. Clean the brush and paint the blue stripe quickly.

"Now there is one more color. We have used the three primary or first colors, so tell me—will this be a primary or an in-between color? Right, in-between. It has to be, because no color is repeated until the start of a new rainbow. The in-between colors are called secondary because they come second, right after the first or primary colors. Now, which primary colors haven't we mixed? Here's the red. We mixed red and yellow to make orange, and we mixed yellow and blue to make green. We have blue left. Has it been mixed with red? No. We'll do that."

Mix the blue and red paint. Say: "What color have I made? It is purple. That makes a complete rainbow. Now I'll paint the last stripe."

While talking, finish painting the rainbow. Then say: "If we wanted to make another rainbow, we'd have to start on top of the red and go backwards to purple again. Which kind of rainbow would you like to paint by yourself? You may make a round one, as you did with the crayons, or one like the one I just painted."

Let the child make as many rainbows as he likes, but be sure he uses his equipment correctly and puts the colors in their proper sequence.

Even though the child may be wholly or partially color-blind, he can learn much from the densities and values of colors. Help him to keep the primary colors in the proper place so he can associate names, actions, locations, movement, and values.

Every parent is inclined to allow a child to "draw what he likes." This is fine, but allow it at some other time. Put the "lesson things" away after each lesson is completed, and at some other period allow him to create his own pictures. This approach will give him a sense of the importance of learning. If suggestions for learning the basic skills are kept "special," the child will understand what learning is and be a more disciplined student. He will know what it means to study, to learn, then to go on to fulfill his tasks and creative projects without fumbling.

Chapter 6

LEARNING TO TOUCH AND FEEL, TASTE AND SMELL

Every child can use his hands, but some can perform more adeptly than others. We can tell this by observing the way babies handle their first toys and picture books, by the ease—or lack of it—with which they hold a cup, spoon, and other utensils.

However, the time this ability becomes most evident is when it is put to the test of using scissors or holding a pencil or crayon. If the child is helped by training his hand muscles, this handling skill can be developed.

AIMS

1. Coordination of the sensory channels.
2. Small muscle control and development.
3. Learning the associate responses received from a variety of stimuli.

PRETEST

1. Can your child grasp and hold objects properly?
2. Can he lift them up, particularly from a slick surface, and set them down in a designated place, without fumbling?
3. Can he hold a scissors or pencil or crayon properly, and move it in a designated direction?
4. Can he turn a door knob to open a door?

Some children learn to perform these activities at an earlier age than others. Do not expect too much from your child at the beginning of the training. Even a very little improvement should be commended, for it is not easy to acquire these new skills, which will be important when the child enters kindergarten or first grade.

MATERIALS NEEDED

1. Blunt scissors and modeling clay.
2. Board or waxed paper; rolling pin or tall glass.
3. Jars and screw-on covers.
4. Tweezers, or any implement that employs the same principle.
5. Buttons, beads, etc.

Activities After you have assembled the materials for clay cutting, work the clay in your hands until it is soft and ready to roll out. On the table, place a board or a sheet of waxed paper on which to put the clay. If you have a rolling pin, use that for flattening the clay. A tall glass or glass jar will serve this purpose as well, or use your hands. Have at hand a container to hold the clay when it is not in use.

Say something like this to the child: "This is modeling clay. It has oil in it so that it won't dry. You can use it over and over again. Since it contains oil, we must be careful not to get it on rugs or furniture; it will make spots.

"We'll keep it in this container when we're not using it. First, we'll roll out the clay like this." Pick up the clay, then add, "Now you can cut this strip into little pieces."

Have him cut as many pieces as he chooses. When his hand is tired, he'll tell you, but be sure to watch for fatigue and stop before he is bored with the activity. As he uses his clay, add other steps; trace around a coin or design made with a simple cookie cutter. Have him cut around the design. As he gains skill, have him make designs of his own—chickens, turkeys, flowers, or anything he can create.

The shapes will not be perfect, but appreciation of his efforts will go a long way to inspire him to make further use of his small muscles. This is good training for the long hours of writing ahead of him.

Use jars with screw tops for the next activity. Call his attention to the fact that all the covers are turned the same way when they are screwed on and the other way when screwed off. Say something like this: "See if you can find a top that goes on the other way," or "Does this one turn the same way?"

Tweezers and small objects are of the greatest interest to a youngster. On a tray, place several small objects of two or more varieties. Say something like this: "Put all the beads in this cup and all the pieces of macaroni in this one and all the buttons in this one." When you use such small objects, watch the child carefully to see that he does not put any of them into his mouth, ears, or nose. Do not allow the child to perform this activity without supervision.

Continue in this way: "If you drop an object, pick it up with your fingers and put it here." Have a less attractive container for the ones that he drops or misses. Say: "See if you can keep this one empty."

If your child would like to have you do this activity with him, to make a game of it, supply yourself with similar objects and containers, give yourself a handicap of a certain number of objects, and start at the same time. Don't be surprised if he will soon not need to have you handicapped.

Supplementary Activities   There are many other games that can be devised and followed for training the small hand muscles. Bolts and nuts are excellent for this purpose. Have the child screw on the nuts, and then screw them off again. He will learn that one must always turn them the same way for putting them on, and the opposite way for taking them off.

The same point can be made by using an old alarm clock—he can turn the hands either way, but the results will be different. Have the child practice turning door knobs and opening and closing drawers. Let him wind string on a spool or piece of cardboard. Old-fashioned tops are good, but rather difficult to obtain; perhaps you can make one by putting a sucker-stick through a milk bottle top. If this is balanced correctly, it can be made to spin.

A large, blunt needle threaded with a length of cord can be used for stringing together short pieces of macaroni, buttons, or other such objects.

Summary and Check   Your child now has learned to do some things that not only have trained his hand muscles, but also have supplied him with activities that will enable him to entertain himself, perhaps for hours at a time. Try him out and see how well he performs and how much he has improved.

To sharpen further the sense of feeling, differences in texture should be taught. Besides learning the meaning of such words as soft, smooth, hard, and rough, and the sensations associated with them, the child should be made aware of the degree to which they exist.

MATERIALS NEEDED

1. Some cotton
2. A stone
3. A piece of smooth glass
4. Some sandpaper

Activities Place the materials on the table in front of the child. Ask the child to touch the cotton and tell you if it is soft or hard. If he doesn't know, say something like this: "The cotton feels soft. What else have you felt that was soft?"

He might name a pillow, your hand, hair, or a dress.

Ask him to feel the stone, and say: "That feels hard. Your hand does not sink into it, the way it did into the cotton. Hard is the opposite of soft. What else is hard?"

He should have no trouble naming things that are hard: furniture, dishes, wood, metal, and so on. Ask him to rub his hand across the surface of the piece of glass. Say something like this: "That feels smooth. Name other things that feel smooth." He may name the furniture again, the dishes, possibly cloth; ask him to tell you which are smooth and hard, which are smooth and soft.

Have the child rub his finger on the sandpaper. Say: "That feels rough. It is the opposite of smooth. Name some other things that feel rough."

He might name the rug, his coat, or the sand on the beach. Ask him to tell you what feels both rough and soft, or rough and hard.

Take this opportunity to call attention to degrees of each of the texture qualities.

Find materials that have different degrees of roughness and

smoothness, softness and hardness. Have him use the words soft, softer, softest; hard, harder, hardest; soft, medium, hard; etc.

The sense of smell is stimulated by contact with gases and vapors emanating from objects or substances. This sense has, first of all, a reaction that gives pleasure or displeasure. Specifically, the odors can be either sweet, sour, spicy, flowery, fruity, resinous, putrid, or burned. A child can learn to distinguish among these odors and, by association, use them to build more complete concepts of what he touches, sees, and hears. Position and distance of objects can sometimes be estimated by the strength of their odor.

However, smell is so closely related to taste that it sometimes cannot be distinguished from it. The taste organs, primarily located on the tongue, must have contact with chemicals before they can be stimulated. Taste can discriminate between sweet and sour; it can perceive salty and bitter flavors; it can produce feelings of hot, cold, and pain. By association, taste sometimes adds to the complete knowledge of what is perceived by the other senses.

The sense of smell, easily fatigued, becomes less acute and finally inoperative if subjected to the same odor for any length of time. Only one whiff should be used when training a child's smelling ability. Some odors, such as orange and gardenia, are complementary and cancel each other out.

AIMS

1. To call attention to the power of taste and odor.
2. To associate tastes and odors with specific substances.
3. To strengthen learning by adding two more sense impressions.

MATERIALS NEEDED

1. Sugar.
2. Vinegar.
3. Salt.
4. A bitter substance (quinine has a genuinely bitter taste; the inside of some fruit seeds, such as those of oranges or peaches, would do.)
5. Cold water and hot water.
6. Containers and spoons.

Activities Put a little of each substance in a container. Use separate spoons when necessary to keep tastes unmixed.

As the child tastes first the sugar, then the vinegar, say something like this: "Is it sweet or sour?" If he does not know which word to use, say: "This is called sweet; this is called sour."

As he tastes the salt, say: "Do you know what this is? Yes, it is salt. It tastes salty."

When he tastes the bitter substance, say something like this: "Do you like that taste? It doesn't taste very good, does it? Sometimes a little bitter taste is pleasant, but too much can be disagreeable. It can be a bad taste."

When he tastes the cold water, then the heated water, ask him whether they are hot or cold. Be sure he uses the correct word for each.

Have the child close his eyes, or blindfold him; let him test the substances again, in a different order. See whether he can identify them as sweet, sour, salty, bitter, hot, and cold.

Ask him to name foods that are sweet. He probably will name cake, cookies, and various desserts. For *sour* he may name pickles or lemons; he might name some kind of nuts or fruit for *bitter*, but if he cannot think of any, help him. The *salty* taste will be easy to learn but hard to associate with specific foods, unless perhaps salted nuts or popcorn. *Cold* naturally would be associated with ice-cream or cold drinks; *hot* with any food or drink that is served hot, as hot chocolate, hot cereal, or soup.

Repeat this activity on different days if he has shown any lack of ability in taste discrimination.

MATERIALS NEEDED

1. A piece of candy, some honey, or some syrup.
2. Vinegar, a sour pickle, or a slice of lemon.
3. Spice, such as cloves or cinnamon.
4. Any fragrant local flower, except a gardenia.
5. An orange.
6. A piece of resin (this may be omitted, if hard to obtain; if there is a pine tree nearby, you may be able to obtain some resin).
7. A freshly burned match, or some ashes.
8. Containers or pieces of waxed paper.

Activities Place the materials in separate containers or on waxed paper. Remember that the child should take only one whiff. Have him smell something sour. Say something like this: "Do you know the name of that smell? Just the smell, is it sweet or sour? Can you name something else that has that same kind of smell, a sour odor?" He may name pickles, various kinds of fruit, or salad dressings.

Sweet is best recognized as the opposite of *sour*. Since the purely sweet odor is hard to isolate, at least two substances should be used. Ask the child to smell one and say something like this: "Does this smell sweet? Is its odor different from the sour one? Yes, it is sweet. Smell this other one too. It is not sour. It is sweet. Many things that don't smell alike can smell sweet. Sweet is the opposite of sour."

Ask him to name other things that smell sweet. He probably will name various desserts, fruits, flowers, or perfumes.

When he smells the spice, tell him that it has a "spicy" odor. Later when the occasion arises, he can learn to discriminate between the different kinds of spice odors.

When he smells the flower, he might say it has a sweet smell. That is all right, but tell him it is a "flowery" odor. Tell him that the fruits are "fruity," but can also be sweet or sour. Actually, after smelling many flowers and fruits, he will soon be able to determine easily their distinctive odors.

The odor of resin may be new to him, but it is different enough to be remembered.

As the child smells the burned match, say something like this: "This is a rather unpleasant odor. It is burned. Many things that are not burned have a disagreeable odor, something like it."

If the child has had occasion to smell any chemicals, cleaning compounds, or decayed substances, he may associate these with the burned or putrid smell.

Have him close his eyes, or blindfold him. Let him try to identify the kinds of odors in different sequences.

There will be many times in a child's life when he can practice naming the different kinds of tastes and smells. He will often associate pleasant tastes and odors with his enjoyment of events and places.

The use of these senses in conjunction with seeing, hearing, and feeling will strengthen learning and make it more complete.

GAMES AND CREATIVE INTERESTS WILL SHARPEN PERCEPTION

Remember that a feeling of accomplishment is very important to a child. To quote an old maxim, "success breeds success." When he does something correctly, praise him if praise is due. Let him do it again to show someone else in the family that he has learned something new—maybe even something that is new to the one for whom he is "showing off."

With repetition and practice in making the right judgment about such basic truths as position, shape, and direction, he will acquire an ability to apply the skills he has learned to subsequent experiences. He will have a feeling of security that will add enjoyment to his learning processes.

Given opportunities to choose between what is right and what is wrong in varying situations, a child becomes logical in his thinking. He will be able to see the patterns in nature, in mathematics, in history, in every subject he will study. Life in general will be less confusing if he can recognize such things as cause and effect, truth and error.

This lesson will be a review of the previous work. Try to make the child feel that he has accomplished something important. If you cannot cover the entire lesson in one day, you can continue with it the next day, or when convenient.

AIMS

1. To make each sense more acute.
2. To bind the senses together into a strong cable for better perception.

3. To develop a sense of responsibility in the child so he will be more cooperative and obedient.

4. To insure greater safety, due to an ability to follow directions.

PRETEST

1. Can the child listen and do at the same time?

2. Can he see and do at the same time? Have the child move his own finger across the cat pictures from the earlier lesson as he moves his eyes from left to right.

3. Can he listen and see at the same time? Have the child look at a picture that includes a variety of objects. Name a particular object, and ask him to look directly at that object.

4. Can he listen and do at the same time? Use the same procedure with the picture, and have him put his finger on the object as he looks at it.

MATERIALS NEEDED

Those already used, plus the new pictures.

Activities There are two old games that combine the skills your child has been using. One is Simon Says, and the other is I Spy.

When you play Simon Says, have the child face you. Say something like this, "This is a game that I played when I was little, and my mother played when she was little, and her mother played when she was little. This is a listening-doing-seeing game. There are three ways to play it. We'll do the easy one first. I'll say 'Simon says thumbs up,' and we'll put our thumbs up.

"Then I'll say 'Peter says thumbs up.' We won't put our thumbs up, because we do that only when Simon says to do it. Are you ready? Listen carefully. Simon says 'thumbs up!' Good. Simon says 'thumbs down!' That's right. Peter says 'thumbs up.' Oh, oh, we can't do it, Simon didn't say it. Simon says 'wiggle waggle.' That's right, we'll move both of our thumbs back and forth."

When this version of the game has become easy for the child, say the directions in various sequences, one after the other, but do not perform the actions, yourself. When he can follow quickly and accurately, explain that in the next game, you will play, too, and you will sometimes do it wrong yourself, so he must listen carefully to what is said, not follow what you do, so that he won't make the same mistake.

I Spy is played with a thimble, a spool of thread, or some other small object about the same size. First demonstrate how you will hide it somewhere in the room; then have him go out of the room, or close or cover his eyes. Place the object at eye level in a rather obvious place the first time. When he is ready, say something like this: "Look all around and see if you can find the thimble. If you get close, I'll say, 'You're warm'; if you get very close, I'll say, 'You're hot!' If you're far away, I'll say, 'You're cold.'"

Each time you play, hide the object so that he can find it, but make the game progressively more difficult so that his faculties will be sharpened. Later, you can vary the game: Say, "Now I'll close my eyes and you hide it. You tell me when I'm hot or cold."

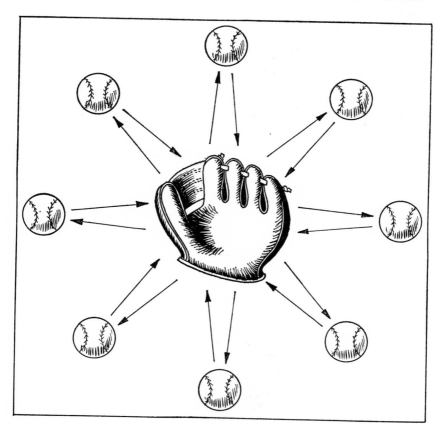

The two diagrams on page 39 and below have been specially designed for you to use to teach the child to follow with his eyes movement both up and down and sideways, but without moving his head.

Place your forefinger in the baseball mitt and tell him that the catcher is going to throw the ball to different fielders. Then follow the flight of the ball as shown by the arrows. Follow the sequence slowly at first, and later somewhat faster; change direction, skipping from side to side. Be sure to watch the child to insure that he moves only his eyes and not his head.

To perfect the up-and-down movement of his eyes, turn to the drawing of the birds. Tell him how mother birds feed their babies and trace the progress of the worm from mother to child, at first slowly and then increasingly faster. Again, you should be sure that only the eyes move.

To sum up: Stress the need for following directions in any game, staying with the right sequence in any stories you read or tell. Make up additional directions to follow, increasing both the speed and the number of instructions he must remember.

Creativity is another area of a child's ability that should be noted. He may have various special aptitudes that permit him to do "better" in particular fields of endeavor. In some children, special interests may tend to take precedence over other areas of learning.

If all a child's senses are trained to operate efficiently, he will be able to develop his talents more effectively and he will be equipped to make use of them throughout his life. Often the recognition of creativity and an opportunity to give it expression lead a child to become more interested in the more common skills.

Becoming adept in all areas of sense perception will give a child the ability to use his special abilities, without taking away any of the spark of individuality that makes him a person in his own right.

Fluency, the ability to move smoothly and easily in a given direction, is closely related to creativity, when applied to evolving something new and different from one's own thoughts and actions. Creativity and fluency may exist in any area, such as words, oral or written; any of the sciences; and arts, mechanics, and humanities.

Wherever the child's interests may lie, he should begin with a clear perception of basic truths and adeptness in basic skills; then his thoughts and actions will have a firm foundation and a starting place from which his ingenuity can be used with fluency to produce good and honest results.

The exercises suggested here will enable you to discover some of your child's special abilities and interests.

AIMS

1. To discover your child's areas of creativity.
2. To discover his interests.
3. To give him an opportunity to show some of his aptitudes.
4. To suggest ways to follow his particular inclinations.

MATERIALS NEEDED

1. Some styrofoam or plastic spheres, half-spheres, and ovoids (egg-shapes). Cubes and other solids, or apples, oranges, or other fruits, various shaped vegetables, blocks.
2. Toothpicks, or other slender sticks.
3. The patterns for making cubes, rectangular solids, and cylinders found in this book.
4. The lists of books and collections accompanying this chapter.
5. Paper and pencil.

Activities   If styrofoam shapes are available, have the child see what he can make out of them. Toothpicks can be used for legs of animals, arms and legs of people, or for fastening a small ball on top of a larger one to make a human head. The half-spheres and egg-shapes can be utilized for creating other objects.

Apples, oranges, or other fruits and vegetables can be used in the same way. For making birds, slits can be put on the sides to hold paper wings. Let the child show his own creativity by carrying out his own ideas.

Buildings, trains, furniture can be constructed from cubes and other shaped blocks.

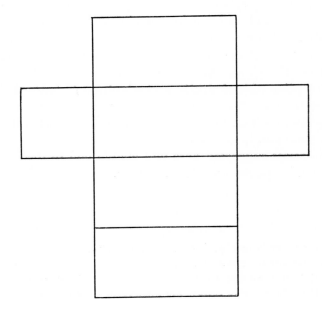

Cones, rectangular solids, and cylinders, made from the patterns supplied in this book, can be used to make furniture, trees, dolls, or anything that comes to the child's mind as he looks at the shapes.

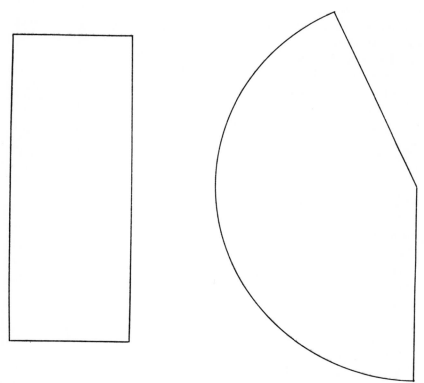

Draw circles on a piece of paper, or have the child draw them by tracing the outline of a round object. Older children may want to use compasses.

Ask the child to see what he can create from the circle base. He might make faces and add ears and hair; he might add heads, legs and arms to make people; he might make a moon or a watch. Have him use his own imagination and creative ability to make anything at all that he can visualize when he looks at a circle.

Follow the same procedure with other shapes, such as ovals, squares, triangles, rectangles.

The child who needs no direction has true creativity. Give him plenty of time to develop his ideas. Try it again another day, and see whether some new thought has come to him.

Creative people are usually sensitive to line, texture, sound, and color. Color is so much a part of our lives that we are likely to let a child pass over the areas that could be enriched by it. To make your child more conscious of color, make a practice of saying such things as, "Bring me the red ball," or "Put the blue bowl out for the beets. I like those colors together."

For a child, there are hours of enjoyment in a box of paint samples to sort and combine. Scarves of pieces of materials to drape for puppets or dolls can serve as the basis for another learning activity; the child can feel the shock of a flaming orange toy-stage curtain as it sweeps away to show a bright blue sky. This will carry him into realms of detail perception in nature and his whole environment. It will inspire him to use color, as well as shape and texture, creatively.

You may want to ask your child some questions that will elicit information about his interests. Yes and no answers are enough for this purpose.

No division need be made between age groups, but those shown may be helpful. Ask one or all of the following questions about the various subjects listed:

"Have you heard stories or poems about any of these?"

"Have you read books, stories, or poems about them?"

"Would you like to hear or read about any of them?"

You may start at the beginning with a child of any age, in order not to miss his particular interest. The younger children may be taken all the way through, if you feel they are interested. Add to the lists of books and collections as many other subjects as you can think of.

As the child answers the questions in any group, you may find the starting point for many conversations with him. If he can write, the questions may suggest topics for paragraphs, compositions, or poems. Some children even attempt to write a book! Go over the lists again when the very young child has advanced to the writing stage. Do not be concerned if he misspells some word, or omits some punctuation. Those errors can be corrected when the time comes.

Preschool Age	First Three Grades	Grades Four through Six
animals	dogs	heroes
birds	horses	history
real people	America	governments
imaginary people	other countries	politics
fairies	sun, moon, stars	weather
angels	trees	religion
Christmas	flowers	buildings
other holidays	fish	art
	cars	mathematics
	airplanes	science
	music	space
		chemistry
		medicine
		family history

Ask your child, "Do you have, or would you like to have collections of any of these?"

Preschool Age	First Three Grades	Grades Four through Six
Pictures of:	cars	records
figures	airplanes	costumes
animals	boats	books
birds	picture cards	magazines
fish	pictures of:	pennants
trees	athletes	flags
fruit	actors	maps
dolls	art	pictures of:
doll furniture	poems	famous people
doll dishes	songs	works of art
miniatures (small	scrapbooks	data concerned with:
objects)		history
buttons		antiques
shells		money
stones		stamps
rocks		mottoes
seeds		
pods		

Some parents may find time to write down what a child says. Some creative children can express poetic and interesting thoughts before they can write them. It is the idea, and the idea alone, that counts at this point.

Chapter **8**

LEARNING POSITION AND DIRECTION OF THE HANDS AND FEET

Knowing position egocentrically—that is, from within one's self —is the first step in recognizing the position of objects which make up one's environment.

This knowledge is important to a child's sense of reality and of security. He should first learn which is his own right and which is his left. We accept the fact that usually right hands, right feet, right eyes, and right ears have dominance over the left. Most of the contrived mechanics of living are arranged with this in mind.

Some individuals, however, have left dominance. Others have mixed dominance. The dominance pattern of a person does not give any indication of his intelligence measurement. Some authorities believe that dominance plays a great part in learning patterns, but others question this. If it is of interest to you, it is very easy to check.

Take a sheet of note paper and fold it twice. At the center fold of the paper, tear out a little piece to make a hole in the center of the paper. Try the following instructions out yourself first, in order to be sure of the sequence.

Using both hands, hold the paper at arm's length straight in front of you. Sight a doorknob through the hole. Close one eye (you can cover the child's eye with your hand if you stand directly behind him.) If you can see the doorknob, check the eye you are using. That is the dominant eye. If you can't see it, try the other eye. If you can see it, that is the dominant eye. (Any deviation, such as seeing two holes, should be checked with your doctor.)

When you have established the child's dominant eye, say to

47

him, "Crumple the paper into a ball and throw it to me." Note which hand he uses to throw it. That is probably his dominant hand, although you should also note which hand he uses for eating, drawing, and other activities. Many children take a long time to establish their preference and certainly they should have plenty of time to do so and not be influenced to use one hand or the other before they are ready.

To test the foot dominance, take the same crumpled ball and drop it in front of him, being careful to center it. Tell him to kick it, and watch to see which foot he uses.

Another way to check eye-hand dominance is to roll a magazine into a tube, securing it with a rubber band. Put it on a table in front of him so he can make a choice of hand and say, "Pretend you are a pirate looking for ships at sea." A child would ordinarily pick it up with the dominant hand and put it to his dominant eye to sight.

The most desirable sequence of dominance is right eye, hand, and foot, since ours is a right-handed world. The next best is a complete left dominance. The mixtures, such as left hand and right eye dominance, are the ones that some reading authorities and doctors are concerned about. If you note a mixture, your doctor can advise you. Without doubt, perception training, such as that in the activities of this section, will be of great value to any child to establish the concepts necessary for learning. It will not only help a mixed dominant, but also the child with straight dominance.

It is unwise to change a child's natural pattern of dominance. Only in rare cases do doctors recommend this. The chances of having a serious crossed dominance problem (or *laterality conflict*, as some doctors call it) are very slight. Your role is to watch and report any unusual differences in the child's pattern of established dominance to your doctor. He will recommend procedures and help you solve the problem if he thinks it is necessary.

The activities that follow are for all children, no matter what their dominance. The more practice he has in perception skills, the better prepared the child will be to attack his first experiences with abstract symbols. The more experience he has with three-dimensional objects, which are the basis for subsequent two-

—is your left side. Everything that is on the right of that—on the same side as your right hand—is your right side. Now point to your right eye, your left eye, your left ear, your right ear. Raise your right arm, your left arm. Do you have a left mouth? No, of course not, that is in the middle, like your nose."

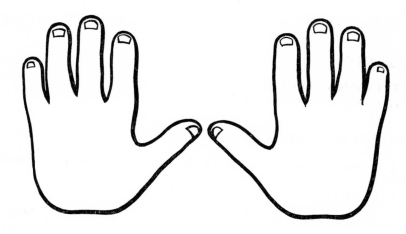

Ask the child to name some objects—furniture or toys—on his left, then on his right. Have him turn around, and do the same thing. Do this until you feel that he knows that his left and right are always in reference to himself, egocentrically; then proceed to other objects that have their own lefts and rights according to the direction they face, and according to their relations with other objects.

Supplementary Activities   Cut out or draw a series of left and right hands and see if the child can point to the correct ones. Cut out shapes of gloves and mittens for the same purpose. The backs of these will have to be marked in some way. Have him point to, or reach into, right and left pockets on himself or on someone else. Use old gloves and mittens for him to try on.

The directions in the next steps employ the left and right foot. The purpose is to help further to establish which is right and which is left. The child can then proceed with greater security to more difficult activities involving position, direction, distance, and speed.

AIMS

1. To know with assurance which is right and which is left.
2. To be able to move to the right or left as directed.
3. To know which objects are to the left and which are to the right.
4. To compare distances of different objects to the right and to the left.
5. To regulate his own speed of movement in walking or marching.

PRETEST

1. Can the child tell his left foot from his right?
2. Can he tell which is a right shoe and which is a left?

MATERIALS NEEDED

1. A piece of paper upon which the child's feet may be outlined, with and without shoes or socks.
2. Paper, crayons, and scissors.

Activities Put a piece of drawing paper on the floor. When you are ready, say something like this: "Yesterday we learned left and right by using the hands. Today we shall use the feet. Put your left foot here on the left side of the paper. We'll trace around it first." Trace around the shoe. "Now put your right foot on the right side of the paper." Trace around the right shoe.

"Now, let's take off your shoes and socks, so I can trace around the shape of your foot. Put your left foot down and I'll draw around the big toe first. Do you notice that your big toe is on the right side of your left foot? That's just like your thumb, when you see the back of your left hand. Now we'll go over and around the other toes, then we'll trace the left side of the foot around the heel, then the right side of the foot back to the big toe.

"We'll do the same thing with your right foot. We'll start with the big toe, over the four other toes, down the right side of the foot, around the heel, then the left side of the right foot, and back to the big toe. Now let's look at the outlines of the feet.

"That's funny. The left foot has a left side and a right side, and the right foot has a right side and a left side. Do you know why? Let's draw a line through the middle of each foot, from the toes to the heels. The part of the left foot that is closest to the right foot is *its* right side, and the part of the right foot that is closest to the left foot is *its* left side. Now let's cut out the feet."

You may have to do some of the outlines over again, if they are not cut out well enough to tell which is the left and which is the right foot! Be patient, as this is not easy. If the child cannot cut them out himself it does not matter; do it for him. Put the shapes on the table, and practice choosing between left and right. Put them on the floor, and have the child match his own feet to them. Put them in the wrong position sometimes, and see if he notices the mistake.

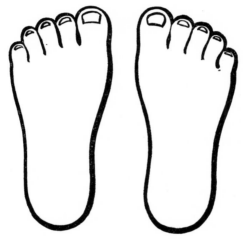

Choosing right and left is something that often takes a child a long time to learn. While he is learning this, he still will love to march. You can use marching music or you can be a "top sergeant" who calls out directions, "*left*, right, *left*, right, mark time, march!" Remember that emphasis on the "left" will help him find the place to start in his book, when he learns to read. If you show him how to mark time or march, be sure that you face in the same direction as he, so as not to confuse him. He will have a lesson later that will show him how the left and right of persons who are facing each other are on different sides.

Supplementary Activities Cut out a series of left and right feet and see if the child can point to the correct ones. Use slippers and shoes for him to line up in pairs. Let him put his feet into slippers and shoes; see if he can choose the correct ones.

Chapter 9

LEARNING DIRECTION

Now that your child has had some training in discerning between left and right, he can go on to the learning of other positions. He probably will have a concept of *front* and *back* and *in* and *out*, but he still needs to establish a quick and easy recognition of these positions. Other words are used that have somewhat the same meaning, such as *before* and *behind, inside* and *outside, into* and *out of.*

There are many little children in kindergarten or first grade who do not know for *sure* what the teacher means when she says such things as, "Look at the front cover of your book," or "Go to the back of the room," or "Put your book *in* your desk, not *on* your desk," or "Face the front of the room." Often a child is considered disobedient or uncooperative when actually he just does not have a clear and definite understanding of position.

AIMS

1. To teach the child the concepts of front and back and in and out, as they relate to himself.

2. To help him to understand these concepts as they relate to things about him.

3. To enable him to follow directions that require an understanding of these concepts.

PRETEST

1. Can the child tell you which is the back and which is the front of his head?

2. Can he distinguish between the front and back of his coat?

3. Can he tell which is the inside and which is the outside of his coat, his shoes, his hat?

4. Can he tell whether he is *in* the house or *out* of the house or a room?

MATERIALS NEEDED

1. Objects around the house.
2. A circle drawn with chalk on the floor or on a paper placed on the floor.

Activities   Place the paper with the circle on the floor where the child can reach it easily with his feet and hands. Look at the picture on page 56 in this book. Say something like this: "Inside the circle is *here.*" Point to the inside of the circle. "We'll call that *in.* Outside of the circle is anywhere beyond; we'll call that *out. Out* is anywhere outside the line that makes the circle." Motion to the area outside the circle.

As you trace the circle with one hand, point with the other and say: "Here is inside—in. Put your foot in the circle. Good. Now put your hand outside the circle. Now we'll do something harder. You'll have to listen carefully because I'll say right or left hand, right or left foot. I'll also say *in* or *out.*

"That's three things to hear, remember, and do. You'll have to make a choice each time. Now put your left foot outside of the circle. Put your right inside of the circle. Good." Repeat directions like these until the child is sure of himself.

If he can do this easily, follow with the next activity. "Now I'm going to add something more since you do this so well. This time you'll do something with a foot and a hand or two feet and two hands. Ready? Put your left foot into the circle and your right hand out of the circle. Now both of your feet out of the circle, and your left hand in the circle."

You will find this easier to direct, if you jot down sequences and combinations to follow. You might also like to keep score, since children like to know how well they have done. This will also give you an idea of where he makes errors, and you can emphasize those points in future practice. He should acquire both speed and accuracy in following the directions. Some children do these things easily while others need much practice.

One step closer to the abstraction of a left and right concept is an activity where you use the hands and feet that were cut out. You could put the outline of the circle on a table or a chair, or leave it on the floor. Take the cut-outs and place the left hands and feet on the child's left, and the right ones on his right. Use the same type of directions.

Look at the picture on this page that shows "back" and "front" and discuss it. To establish the concept of front and back, start with the hands. Say: "Show me the backs of your hands; now the fronts. The front is really more important than the back. You feel things with the front. Get me a book and let me show you something about its front and back. The front of most books has the name on it. The way to tell if you have the book right side up is this. Do you see where the pages are held together? That is the binding, and it must always be on your left, with the name of the book facing you. Now get another book and see whether you can show me the front."

This may take more practice than you expect. It is especially difficult if you have not sorted the books with which you are working. Some books may not have a name on the front cover. The child cannot read, so you'll have to show him the names. Magazines have pictures and printing on both front and back. You will have to help him to find the front. He will eventually be able to do it by himself.

Supplementary Activities and Suggestions   Many other activities can be contrived. Arrange chairs in a row and have the child walk in and out around them. Have him name objects in front of him, then turn his head and name some that are back of him.

Check Test   Ask the child the questions given at the beginning of this lesson. Ask him other similar questions regarding positions. Ask him to stand in front of the door; when he has come back to you ask him to stand behind the door. Ask him to turn his back to you. See whether he follows the directions readily and accurately.

Now is the time to go on to the concepts of *up* and *down.* Many other words are used to express the same general meaning of these concepts—*over* (or *on*) and *under, top* and *bottom, above* and *below.* Each set of words has a little different connotation and will be used accordingly. This lesson, like the others on position and direction, is very important in establishing a sense of orientation in the child. It will help him to know just where he is in relation to his surroundings.

AIMS

1. To establish the concepts of *up* and *down.*
2. To help the child learn which words have the same general meaning as *up* and *down.*
3. To enable him to follow directions that include these concepts.

PRETEST

1. Can the child look up and down as directed?
2. Can he put something on the table, then under the table?
3. Can he hold an object over his head, if asked to do so?
4. Can he hold it above his head but not directly over it?
5. Can he put a piece of paper under his foot, as directed?
6. Can he climb up some steps, then down as directed?
7. Can he tell which way is up and which is down?

MATERIALS NEEDED

1. Objects around the house.
2. Cut-out hands and feet.

Activities The concepts of *up* and *down* can be acquired by starting with a designated object or place; from this starting place, one may make a choice of going up or going down.

Suppose you choose a table top as the starting place. Say to the child: "Let's go to the table with the cut-out hands and feet. If I put them on the table, and then take one and hold it here"—lift it a short distance above the table—"has it gone up or down? Up, of course; it's above the table. Now watch." Move it still higher. "Did it go up or down? That's right. Up. If you move something and it goes higher than it was, it went up. If you move something lower than it was, it goes down. Now take the right cut-out hand from the table and move it up. Is it above the table? Yes. You moved it *up*. Now, take a left cut-out foot, and move it below the table top. Is it lower than the table top? Then you moved it *down*.

"Listen carefully now. Take a left cut-out foot and a right one. Put the right foot above the table, and put the left one below the table. Is the right foot below the table? No? Good. Where is the right foot? Above. That's right. Now tell me, which foot is higher than the other? It's the foot you moved up. Which is it—the right? Good. Which foot is lower than the other? Yes, the left."

You can add more and more ideas, such as: "If those feet were on steps, which would you move to go up? To go down? Which is higher or lower now?" The child should try to visualize steps, or he can look at the picture of the ladder on page 60 of his book. If he actually climbs steps, supervise him. Climbing gives him excellent practice in seeing and estimating distances while moving.

For further training, take three or four objects and place them at various levels around the room. You could use the cut-out hands and feet. Say: "Bring me all the things that are placed higher than your knees. Take the things that are lower than your knees and place them so that they are higher than the ones that are higher than your knees." See if he remembers the position or height of the first group. "Did you move these objects up or down?"

Vary these activities with others that use the concepts of *back* and *front*. "Is the object behind you higher or lower than the one in front of you?" Have the child answer this while looking at the objects. He can turn his head to see. Next time, have him turn himself around, and see if he can recall the position of the object that was in front of him.

Supplementary Activities   Use similar directions with other objects.

Check Test   Give the child the instructions suggested by the questions in the pretest. See whether he can follow them without hesitation. Have him look at the picture on page 60 again, and ask him, "Which foot must the boy on the ladder move to go up? Which to go down?" Ask other questions about how the hands and feet must be moved to go all the way up and all the way down.

Direction can be further established by working with spirals. These activities will train both the hands and the eyes to move from left to right and around from right to left, but more importantly, they will train the child to make judgments of direction, visually and physically.

By identifying his position with the starting point in the center of the spiral, or at the outside end of the line, he can establish an egocentric feeling of position and from there go on to a sense of the right movement to make to correspond with the required direction.

AIMS

1. To attain a sense of position and direction.
2. To make a choice based on sure judgment.
3. To use the eyes and hands correctly.
4. To recognize similarities and differences.

PRETEST

1. See whether the child can tell by looking at the center of a spiral whether he should move his eyes to the left or right to follow the line to its end.

2. Have him move his finger through the air in the direction he thinks the line goes.

3. Have him move his eyes at the same time, and see whether the eye movement follows that of the finger.

MATERIALS NEEDED

The pictures of spirals shown in this chapter.

Activities   Read the directions before you have the child begin. Put the pictures on the table in front of him.

Say something like this: "A spiral is a line that goes around and around, but doesn't touch at any point. It does not close. Put your finger on the dot at the center of the first spiral. Move it to follow the line. Does it start toward the right or the left? It starts by going to the left. Follow the line all the way around. Now, start at the end of the line that makes the same spiral. Which way do you have to move your finger now? Yes, to the right.

"Let's trace the next spiral. That's it, move from the center around to the right. Starting at the end and going back, it goes to the left.

"Try the straight-lined spiral, this one. Start at the center and go around, yes, to the right. Start at the end, and go around to the left.

"Do the next one. Start at the center and go around to the left. Start at the end, and go around to the right.

"Look at the next row of spirals. See if you can tell me which direction they each go. Yes, left, right, right. Which spirals go in the same direction? Which one is different? Try the next row. Which spirals go in the same direction? Which one is different?"

If the child cannot give the correct answers to questions about the spirals in the last two rows, or hesitates too long before giving the answers, let him trace them, then try again. He may have to do this several times.

Turn the pictures around in different positions and let him try to give the directions in which the lines proceed. Ask him each time to tell you which one is different.

Supplementary Activities   Make additional spirals on a piece of paper or on a blackboard and have the child identify the direction in which they are made. Check from the center and from the end of each spiral.

Check Test   Use the same pictures and other pictures to check the child on other days. See if eventually he can give the correct answers instantly, with no hesitation. Be sure to use some entirely different pictures to make sure the answers are not given from memory. Use spirals made in the shape of ovals, triangles, rectangles and any other forms.

Chapter 10

SKILLS NEEDED BY
A CHILD

All the training so far has been involved with the child's everyday living. The same skills are needed as a child learns to dress himself, when he learns to eat properly, when he plays games, when he does chores—in fact, they are important in everything he does. They will be used incidentally in future lessons, and they will be used specifically in this lesson, which is in the nature of a review of what he has learned so far and his ability to use all his skills at the same time.

AIMS

1. To insure the use of the senses, separately and together.
2. To make certain that the child's perception is fast and accurate.
3. To give him an opportunity to respond to directions that demand the use of a variety of skills in different combinations.
4. To make sure that he retains and can recall what he has learned.
5. To give him a feeling of security and accomplishment, because of his smooth, fast, and accurate performance.

PRETEST

1. Does the child follow directions?
2. Does he move his eyes properly, without turning his head?
3. Is he adept at using his hands?
4. Does he know which is left and which is right?
5. Does he know the concepts of back and front, in and out, up and down?
6. Can he move himself and various objects in those directions, as directed?

See whether you can answer all these questions affirmatively. If not, wait until you have completed this lesson. Then try again.

MATERIALS NEEDED

Those things you have already used.

Activities Children love to clap hands in rhythm. If you sit facing your child, preferably at his level, he not only will reinforce his recognition of left and right, but also will find great pleasure in participation.

When you are seated, have him tell you which is his right hand and right knee, and which is his left hand and left knee; tell him which is your right and left hand and knee.

Then say something like this: "Let's learn to clap together. See my hands, one on each knee? We'll start there, then clap like this." Demonstrate with your own hands, first putting them on your knees, then clapping them.

"Put your hands on your knees, then clap them together as I did. We'll do it together. On the knees, clap, then touch my left hand with your right hand and my right hand with your left hand at the same time. When we touch each others' hands, we'll say 'double clap.' Again—knees, clap, double clap, knees, clap, double clap."

When the child can do this easily, proceed to another step. "Let's do it a little differently this time. Listen carefully. There will be something new. Knees, clap, cross arms to clap our right hands together, clap our own hands together, then cross arms again to clap our left hands together, then clap our own hands together again. Now we'll do it as I say the words. Knees, clap, right clap, clap, left clap, clap."

Repeat this until the child has learned it. "Now we'll put the whole thing together." Go through both routines by yourself first, with the child paying close attention. "Knees, clap, double clap, knees, clap, double clap, knees, clap, right clap, clap, left clap, clap, double clap, knees."

This may take several sessions and careful rote learning, but it is invaluable for left and right hand training.

To further establish position, direction, and listening to and following instructions, there is nothing better than marching. Say something like this: "Listen carefully. I'm going to tell you exactly how to march. Stand straight and tall like a soldier, head high, chest out, arms at your sides. When I say 'left,' take a step with your left foot; when I say 'right,' take a step with your right foot. Ready? Forward, march, left, right, left. Stop! Put your right foot beside your left foot.

"Now look around and see if you can go back the same distance without bumping into anything. Listen first. I'll say 'go' when it's time to start. And 'stop' or 'halt' when it's time to stop. Ready? Go! Back, right, left, right. Halt! Put your left foot beside your right foot." You may do this as many times as you both care to do so.

Marching forward, of course, is good training at any time, not only for the reasons listed above, but also for assuring controlled motion with estimation of distance by sight.

An activity for improving visual perception is this one, which children generally love. This is invaluable for peripheral vision training—that is, for increasing the child's ability to see things from the corner of his eyes when he is looking straight ahead.

Arrange three chairs or stools in a row, two or three feet apart. On each seat place an object. Choose objects that are not alike and that can be seen readily, such as a book, a pitcher, and a teddy bear or similar toy. Have the child walk behind you, looking directly at your heels. Walk slowly past the chairs and have him stop with his back to them. Ask him to tell you what he saw on the chairs. He may not repeat the names of the objects in order. If this happens, help him to start with the last thing he saw, then the middle one, then the first. It is also good to have him name them in the opposite sequence—first, middle, and last.

It will be much more difficult for him if you ask him to name the middle one first, then the one on the right as he faces them, and then the one on the left. Turn the chairs around and have him go down the line in the same way. Many children can do this best with the objects on their right. Others can do it best when the objects are on their left. Practice will enable the child to become much more visually acute. A double row of chairs with well-defined objects is another step in this training; before you ask him to do it, try it yourself to adjust the degree of difficulty.

Skipping is an activity that helps to establish and reinforce rhythmic dominance patterns. To help your child learn to become better in skipping, work with him as early as he is interested in the activity.

By holding his hand and having him place his feet as you do, then giving him verbal instructions to follow you, he will soon be able to have a perfect skipping rhythm. Say something like this:

"Take hold of my hand. Put your weight on your left foot, lift your right foot; now hop once on your left foot, put your right foot down, life your left foot, hop on your right foot. Again—left hop, right hop, left hop, right hop, etc."

If your child has difficulty, try going to his other side and have him start with his other foot. The dominance pattern in the child may be the opposite of yours and this may confuse him.

Continue to train the eyes for a few minutes every day. Then watch them as the child looks at books, etc., and later on when he starts to read. Repeat the training if he still turns his head, or if his eyes do not seem to be moving smoothly and quickly in the required directions. Give him instructions for doing things in sequence every now and then, so that he does not lose his skill in listening and paying attention. In everyday routines, emphasize the use of words that indicate position and direction, so that he will retain his knowledge of them. Play games with blocks made from the patterns on pages 73, 76 and 80.

Check Test   Now see whether you can answer "yes" to the questions asked in the pretest!

LEARNING SHAPES
AND SHAPE COMBINATIONS

Every solid has shape. There are objects all around us to see and to feel. By seeing and feeling, we can come to know shape. The most fundamental of all shapes is that of a sphere. The earth itself and the heavenly bodies are approximate spheres. A perfect sphere is a satisfying shape. It is uncomplicated and simple, and therefore appealing to a child. He can put his hands around it and feel its roundness. It is comfortable to hold and to catch; it will roll easily and smoothly.

A cube is a little more complicated shape, because it has edges and points. It is still satisfying, because it has the sameness of equal proportions.

Let us begin with spheres and cubes.

AIMS

1. To give training in space relationships.
2. To make logical choices.
3. To make patterns using an orderly arrangement.
4. To give practice in recognizing sequences.

PRETEST

1. Can the child tell which objects are spheres (balls) and which are cubes (blocks)?
2. Can he sort them and line them up according to shape and size?
3. Can he match the ones that are the same shape and the same size? In matching the size, he should be able to match the big sphere and cube, the little sphere and cube, etc.

67

4. Can he estimate distances between them? He should be able to place two objects the same distance apart as the distance between two other objects.

5. Can he make patterns with the spheres and cubes? These patterns should be orderly arrangements in the form of circles, squares, triangles, or straight lines alternating the shapes and sizes. There should be some semblance of a design in the patterns.

A child would not be expected to be able to do most of these things without having had some training. If he can, he has a natural aptitude for them. If he can't, he needs the training. Either way, the training will help him.

MATERIALS NEEDED

1. Three spheres.
2. Three cubes. Have three different sizes for each. Try to have the big sphere approximately the same size as the large cube and the middle-sized ones about halfway between.

Activities   To be at ease and successful in what is known in schools as a "reading readiness" program, a child must be able to perceive likes and differences in areas such as shape, size, and sequence. If he has had the experience of making logical choices when handling three-dimensional objects, he will find it easier to face similar choices when working with two-dimensional figures and finally with abstract ideas.

When he can recognize and match spheres and cubes according to size and sequence of size, he has taken one step toward that goal; if he can add to that the experience of making speedy, accurate selection of designated shapes, he will have acquired an inner sense of likes and differences in size, shape, and sequence.

Place the suggested material—three spheres and three cubes— on a table in front of the child. Say something like this as you point out the spheres: "Here are some objects that are round. They are like balls, but you may call them spheres as the high school boys and girls do. Here's how you can tell a sphere. Put your hands around it, like this. Feel how round it is? You can feel almost every part of your hand against it. Your hands fit around it and, no matter which way you turn the sphere, your hands still fit around it the same way."

Next hand him one of the cubes—the one nearest in size to the sphere he has been handling. "Can you fit your hands around this smoothly? No, the corners stick out and you can't close your hand closely around it. When you feel the corners and edges, you know this is not a sphere. You may call this a block or a cube. Spheres are like balls with no corners or edges; cubes are like blocks with both corners and edges.

"Put all of the spheres on top of the table on the right side; put all of the cubes on the left side. Good. Now listen carefully. Put the largest sphere and the largest cube in the middle of the table. Put the smallest sphere and the smallest cube on the floor. What do you have left? That's right, the middle-sized sphere and cube.

"Next let's make patterns. Put all of the objects on the table. Now take the biggest sphere and put it directly in front of you. Take the biggest cube and put it on the right of the sphere. Listen carefully. Take the middle-sized sphere and place it on the left beside the large sphere. Take the middle-sized cube and put it on the right beside the large cube. Now where do the little cube and the little sphere belong?"

See whether the child places the small sphere at the left of the spheres, and the small cube at the right of the cubes, to form a sequential pattern according to size and shape. If he does not, show him how it should have been done and stress the order from the center out: "Cubes—big, middle-sized, little (or big, smaller, smallest). Spheres—big, middle-sized, little, (or big, smaller, smallest.)"

Various patterns, using the concepts of *above* and *below, in* and *out, right* and *left,* in sequences of both size and shape can be made. The combinations are numerous, and working with them will give the child the experience he needs to assure recognition of size, shape, position, and sequence.

Supplementary Activities Perhaps the child can find round stones or blocks in more than three sizes, or several of the same size. He can sort these, putting them into boxes or containers, or arrange them into different patterns. Play games using blocks made from patterns on pages 73, 76 and 80.

Check Test   Test the child by giving him cubes and spheres to sort according to shape and size. Have him make patterns by placing them in order—big, middle-sized, little, and vice versa.

Circles, squares, curved lines, and straight lines are natural outgrowths of spheres and cubes. They are one step closer to the symbols that represent the abstract meaning of letters and numbers. A child who is able to distinguish easily the similarities and differences of shape and size possessed by these symbols, and to recognize their poitions, is ready to grasp their meaning quickly and easily. They will no longer seem a senseless jumble of marks across a page, but will be a series of shapes put into sequential patterns that have purpose. That is one reason for this lesson. Another reason is the further development of the security that comes from logical, orderly thinking.

AIMS
1. Recognition of shapes.
2. Discovering similarities and differences.
3. Learning to sort, match, and measure.
4. Learning how to think logically by making patterns.
5. Acquiring the ability to pick up flat objects.

PRETEST
1. Can the child identify circles and squares?
2. Can he tell which given lines are straight and which are curved?
3. Can he sort objects according to shape and size?
4. Can he pick up the flat objects easily?

MATERIALS NEEDED
1. Three squares of three sequential sizes.
2. Three cubes of three sequential sizes.
3. Pencil and paper for making straight and curved lines.

Activities   Moving from three- to two-dimensional figures sometimes causes confusion for the child. If you have both of the groups and use them together in the beginning, this confusion will be illuminated. To review the concepts of spheres and cubes, say something like this:

"Remember how to tell a sphere from a cube?" Let him tell you if he can; if not, just go on and explain, "Put your hands around the sphere to see whether your hands can touch all around the curved surface. When you turn the sphere, your hands still fit the curve. You may not reach all the way around some big spheres, and your hands may overlap on small ones, but if your hands were the right size they would fit around any sphere. Now can you tell me about a cube? That's right, your hands do not fit smoothly around those corners. Put all the spheres here on the left, and put the cubes on the right."

If you wish to do so, you can demonstrate how circles and squares may be made by taking a sphere and a cube modeled from clay and slicing them. Slice the sphere (an orange could be used) through the middle, and then cut off a slice. This is a circle. Slice the cube to make squares. Whether you perform this demonstration or not, the next step is to show the child the circles and squares that have been assembled.

Say: "Look at these new things. Can you sort them so that the ones that are round like the spheres are next to the spheres, and the ones that are square like the cubes are next to the cubes? Can you tell me how the spheres and circles are alike? That's right, they are round; you can put your hands smoothly around them. How are the squares like the cubes? Yes, they have corners." Be sure that the child feels the figures as you talk about them.

"Now let's mix them all again. Then we'll play a game. Look at the table." Point to the corners. "There is a corner next to you on your left, and one on your right. There is a corner away from you on the right, and one away from you on your left. Now I'll tell you what to do. Find all the spheres and put them in the left corner away from you; put the cubes in the left corner near you, the circles in the right corner away from you, and the squares in the right corner near you."

Give the instructions slowly, so the child will have time to think about them.

Another activity can be performed by matching the spheres and circles according to size, then the cubes and squares according to size. Put the big sphere and circle together, then the middle ones, then the small ones. Do the same with the cubes and squares.

Put the spheres and cubes away and work with the circles and squares. Say something like this: "Place the large circle in front of you, put the middle-sized circle at its right, and put the smallest circle at the right of that. Below the large circle place the large square. Now put the other squares in the same order as the circles."

See whether the child has placed the middle-sized square below the middle-sized circle and the small square below the small circle. Have him place them in reverse order, beginning with the smallest. Next, put the large square on the top, the middle one below it, and the small one at the bottom. Have him put the small circle below that and see whether he continues the pattern by putting the middle-sized circle below the small one and the large one on the bottom. If he does not, show him how it should be, then try it again. Take the large circle, put the large square beside it, then see if he can finish the pattern—middle-sized circle, middle-sized square, small circle, small square.

Put the middle-sized circle about six inches to the right of the big circle and the small one about three inches to the right of that. Ask him to place the squares about the same distance apart on another part of the table. If he does not do this with reasonable accuracy, have him try it again. When he has improved his ability to estimate distance with his eyes, place the circles at varying distances, cover them with a paper, and see whether he can recall the pattern and match it with the squares.

Supplementary Activities Ask the child to find objects that are circles or squares—tops of cans, plates, saucers, parts of furniture.

Have the child draw straight lines using a ruler of cardboard as a guide. Curves can be made by drawing part way around lids of jars, plates or pans. Point out that the stright line is like the edge of a cube and he can *feel* its straightness with his fingers if he traces either the line he has drawn or the edge of a cube. In the same manner he can *feel* a curve and cup his hand to make it match as he can cup his hands about a ball.

Ask him to find straight lines and curves in objects he sees in the house and outdoors. Perhaps he has found round shells at the beach. Call his attention to round cookies and candies. Look for square windows, etc. Use coins, counters or poker chips for practice in picking up objects. Let the child sort buttons according to size. Play games with blocks made from the patterns shown on pages 73, 76 and 80.

Check Test Give the child a quick test by holding up various shapes. See whether he can identify them without hesitation. Put the circles on the left then on the right side of a square, and see whether he can tell which side it is on. Put a square or circle above, then below a horizontal line, and see whether he can tell you its position.

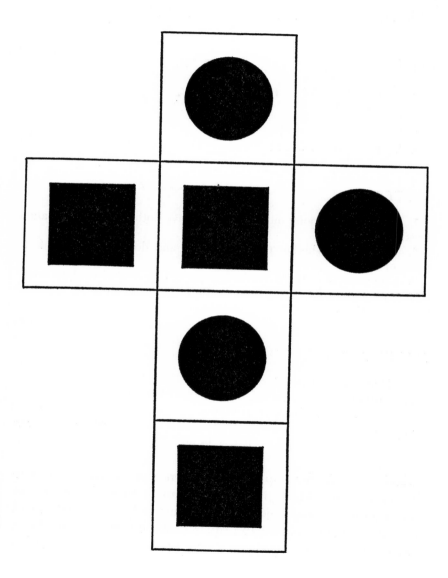

Many objects have shapes that contain both curves and straight lines. In this lesson, we shall look at three-dimensional figures to discover some of these lines. Some curves, of course, will not have the same roundness as that of those in a circle; some straight lines will be slanted in different directions. Your child will be asked to distinguish between curved and straight lines. He will also be asked to tell the position and direction of the lines.

AIMS

1. To perceive likes and differences.
2. To recognize position, direction, and shape readily.
3. To recall concepts presented previously.
4. To assure retention.
5. To make use of what has already been learned.

PRETEST

1. Can the child point out objects that have both curved and straight lines?
2. Can he tell whether the lines go up and down, go from left to right, or slant?
3. Can he make pictures or designs using curved and straight lines? The child should do better now on these pretests, since he has had training in movement, position, direction, and shape.

MATERIALS NEEDED

1. Objects already used.
2. Cartons, cans, tableware, objects around the house.
3. Kitchen utensils of various shapes.
4. Three-dimensional shapes that can be made of paper (patterns for these are to be found on pages 42 and 43.)

Activities To develop a stronger sense of logical analysis in the child, he should be given an opportunity to work with three- and two-dimensional objects that are made by combinations of spheres and cubes, circles and squares, curved and straight lines.

Place three of the objects on a tray (or on the table)—perhaps a large sphere, a medium-sized circle, and a small sphere. Have the child look at them carefully. Say something like this: "Look at these objects because I'm going to have you close your eyes. While your eyes are closed I'm going to change them around, and then you must open your eyes and try to put them back the way they are now. Ready? Close your eyes."

Exchange the first and last. Then say: "All right, open your eyes. Look carefully. Now put them back the way they were before." If he can do it, say: "Good, now we'll make a different pattern." Continue this with different objects.

If he cannot do it, let him make his own pattern before he closes his eyes. As he does it, have him repeat as he places the objects: "The large sphere on the left, the middle-sized circle next—" and so on. This will give the child the necessary training for recall, if visual perception is not enough.

This activity can be varied. The next time use cubes and squares, then mix all the shapes. As he becomes successful, add more and more to the sequence. Here is a good time for the child to learn to space objects. Have him put them a hand-width apart, then three, two, and one finger-width apart. Later, when he begins to write, this will help him to space his letters and words.

If the child persistently misses in a particular part of the sequence—the left, or right, or center—emphasize that spot with an exaggeration, such as a fork in place of a spoon, or a paperclip in place of a safety pin; then go back to the original and see whether he has improved.

When he is able to pick out the "different" one quickly, vary the sequences with some that are correct—that is, with some that have no differences. Since there will be none to point out, he can simply say: "All the same."

Supplementary Activities In everyday life, there are many times when the child will have occasion to notice the shapes of various objects that he sees or touches—for example, his books, pencils, crayons, candy bars, ice cream cones, buildings, trees, plants, flowers, leaves, shells, etc. The size, shape or contour, and position of these can be called to his attention. The important thing is that he has acquired an innate feeling for shape, size, position, and direction.

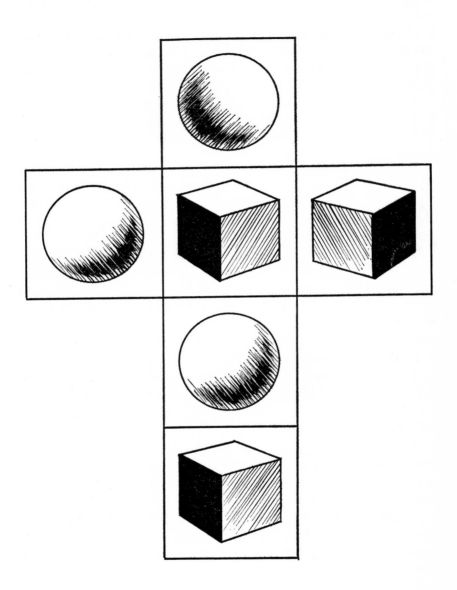

Check Test

1. Have the child identify the curves and straight lines in objects and pictures. See whether he can do this speedily and accurately.
2. See whether he can name objects in order of their sizes—big, in-between, and small. Next, ask him to begin with the small object and proceed to the largest.
3. Ask him to look at the width of a window or a door; then have him place two chairs or other objects so that the distance between them will be equal to that width.

Now that the importance of shape has been covered in a series of activities, all of them designed for perception training, it is advisable to review the previous lessons before going on to the following sections.

After this review, your child will move into the area of combinations of shapes, finding similarities and differences, and making patterns, all these new tasks being connected, of course, with recognizing position, direction, and shape.

AIMS

1. To pay attention.
2. To listen and hear instructions in proper sequence.
3. To follow instructions in the given sequence.
4. To apply previously learned concepts.

PRETEST

1. Does the child hear and listen well?
2. Does he pay attention?
3. Can he follow instructions?
4. Can he move his eyes properly?
5. Can he use his hands well?
6. Does he know right and left?
7. Does he know in and out, back and front, up and down?
8. Can he sort objects according to similarities and differences in shape and size, and perhaps color?
9. Can he arrange objects in rows according to size, shape, and color?
10. Can he place objects in orderly patterns?
11. Can he tell if objects are at the right or left, or above or below a given line?

If you cannot answer all these questions now, observe the child's performance. For when he can do these things, he will be ready for the vitally important lesson that will bring him a step closer to the recognition of symbols that have abstract meaning—that is, the letters of the alphabet and the digits (numbers 1–9.) Words and numbers, of course, are merely letters and digits in meaningful patterns.

MATERIALS NEEDED

1. Three spheres and three cubes.
2. A glass jar.
3. A cone (a paper one will do.)
4. A tin pie pan.
5. A straight-handled spoon.
6. A rectangular-shaped box.
7. A round plastic bowl.

Activities   First, put the spheres and cubes on the table; let the child look at them, then blindfold him. Say something like this: "Hand me the biggest sphere (or ball). Hand me the smallest cube (or block); now the middle-sized cube; now the smallest sphere."

Continue in any irregular sequence, until he has handed you all the objects. Let him feel and compare them as much as necessary. After you have returned them to their place in front of him, have him follow a different procedure. Let him pick out any one and hand it to you. Say: "Is that a sphere or a cube? Is it the biggest, smallest, or middle-sized sphere (or cube)?"

This can be done with the circles and squares also. Now clear the table and put the other six objects in front of him. He should not be blindfolded for this.

Say: "Give me the object that has all straight lines and corners." This will be the box.

"Give me the one that is round and almost flat like a circle." This will be the pie tin.

"Give me the one that is partly straight and partly curved." This will be the spoon.

"Now the one that is partly round but has straight slanted sides."
This will be the cone.

"Now give me the one that is like part of a sphere." This will
be the bowl.

"Now the one that is partly round, but flat on the top and bottom." This will be the cylinder (jar).

If he cannot do this readily, let him feel them and help him
decide which parts are curved and which are straight or flat.

Have him try it blindfolded once he is sure of the shapes of the
objects.

For another activity, have the child examine different pieces
of furniture and answer questions like this:

"Is there anything like a square on the couch?"

"Is there any part of it that is round?"

"Can you touch the corners of that table?"

"Are there any parts of the chair that go across from left to
right?"

"Are there any parts that go up and down?"

"Can you show me any curves on the lamp?"

Ask any questions that fit your furniture, and continue until
the child (or you) are tired of the activity.

Add something like this: "Point out all the straight lines you can
see. Which is the longest line (or distance)? Which is the shortest?
Can you find one that is about the same length as your arm from
your elbow to the tops of your fingers? Show me the largest chair;
the smallest. Find some curved lines."

Have the child step off distances, putting one foot directly
ahead of and touching the other. After he has done this, see if
he can guess whether certain short distances are equal to one or
both of his feet. If this is done with a child who can count, he
could, of course, estimate longer distances in this way.

Supplementary Activities If the child can draw and cut out
shapes, he will like to spend quiet periods of time with paper,
pencil, crayons, and scissors. Two circles and four straight lines
will make a drawing of a person if placed in the right pattern.
Show him the right proportions if he cannot yet recognize them
himself. Animals, houses, and trees can be made in proportionate
sizes. He can cut out circles and squares. Help him to make his
own blocks and cones by following the patterns on pages 42 and 43.

Check Test

Try again to answer the questions given in the pretest.

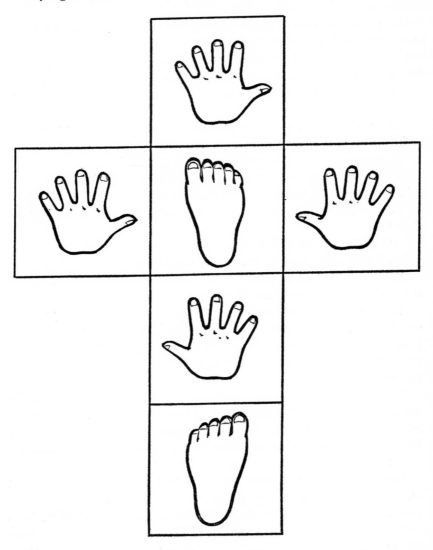

In this chapter, you will find three patterns with the aid of which you can convert a child's play block into a useful teaching aid—and an amusing game as well.

The designs should be traced onto stout paper, then cut out and mounted on a wooden block.

You can then roll the various blocks and have the child call out "right foot," "left hand," "sphere," "cube," "square," "circle," or whatever appears on the top of the blocks.

You will find that you are able to play this game for quite a long time before the child loses interest in this painless way to acquire knowledge.

Chapter 12

SHAPES USED FOR SYMBOLS

These lessons are concerned with the straight and curved lines used to make lower-case letters. Still another series includes number digits; those, however, have concepts that go beyond this training. It is not necessary at this stage for the child to know the names or values of the symbols, which will be discussed in later chapters.

If he knows the names of the letters, it is all right for him to call them by name; there is no harm in your telling him their names. Children who have already learned to make the letters would also profit by this lesson. So often, they do not learn to make them properly: They use curved instead of straight lines, and vice versa; they slant lines too much or not enough; and, most harmful to their future learning of letters and words, they reverse letters. The letters most often reversed or made backwards are the *b* and the *d*, the *g* and the *p*, and the *k*, the *s*, and the *z*.

AIMS

1. To review and apply the concepts of position, shape and size.
2. To establish greater control of the small muscle control necessary for making abstract symbols.
3. To coordinate eye-hand perception channels.

PRETEST

1. Can the child tell whether a circle or curved line is on the left or right side of a line, as in *a, b, d, f, g, j, m, n, p, q, r,* and *u?*

2. Can he tell whether a vertical line is above or below a horizontal line, as in *b*, *d*, *f*, *g*, *h*, *j*, *k*, *p*, *q*, and *y*?

3. Can he tell whether a line is curved to the right or to the left, as in *c*, *f*, *g*, *h*, *j*, *r*, and *s*?

This test can be given by using the letters printed on page 93.

MATERIALS NEEDED

1. Letter-shapes. To make them, you can cut out paper in the shapes pictured on page 96.

2. Illustrations of letter-shapes.

abcdefg

hijklmno

pqrstuv

wxyz

Activities Have the child look at the row of letter-shapes. Draw a line under the shapes so the lower part of the *g*, *j*, *p*, *q*, and *y* will show below. Call his attention to the fact that the shapes are all made of circles, curved lines, and straight lines. You may call the horizontal line on which they rest a shelf or ledge. Say something like this: "Put your finger on each of the whole circles." The complete circles are those that are used in *a, b, d, g, o, p,* and *q.*

Then say: "Are any of the circles below the shelf? No. Are any of them above the shelf? That's right, all of them are above the line. Which are on the right side of the lines that go up and down? Which are on the left of the lines that go up and down?

"Put your finger on all the tall straight lines that are above the shelf." He should touch the lines of the *b, d, h, k, l,* and *t.* If he touches the *f,* that is all right. Show him how the line curves down to the right on the top, and have him trace it with his finger.

"Now put your finger on the long lines that go below the shelf. That's right." He should touch the *g, p, q,* and *y.* "Which of those curves up to the left?" (The *g* shape.)

"Which has a line slanting down to the left?" (The *y.*) "Which have short lines that go straight up and down?" He should put his finger on the *a, h, i, m, n, r,* and *u.*

"Which short lines go left and right?" They are in the *f, t,* and *z.*

"Which short lines slant to the left?" These are in the *k, v, w, x,* and *z.*

"Which short lines slant to the right?" These are in the *k, v, w, x,* and *y.*

"Which shapes are almost a whole circle?" These are the *c* and *e.*

"Do these face to the right or to the left?" The right, of course.

"Which has a curved shape that faces to the right, and one that faces to the left?" This is the *s.*

"Which have curved shapes with straight edges facing down?" These are the *f, h, m, n,* and *r.*

"Which have curved shapes with straight edges facing up?" These are the *g* and *j.* "Are they above or below the line? Do the lines curve to the right or to the left?" Have the child trace the curves with his finger.

"Can you find some dots? Are they over or below the shapes?" He should put his finger above the *i* and *j.*

Take the shapes and lines that you used earlier. Have the child look at them. Call his attention to what they are. There is a circle, a part of the same-sized circle, a curved shape (which can be turned either way for *f, g, h, j, m, n, r,* and *u*), a curved shape for the *s,* a long straight line, and a shorter straight line. These six shapes and lines will make all the letter-shapes. Actually, there will be some discrepancies, for instance, in matching the short cross lines on the *t* and *f* and the lines in the *k*, *d*, and *t*. Necessary adjustments can be made by folding the strips.

Have the child trace around all these shapes and lines with his finger; then have him trace around the letter-shapes, which he has already studied. As he does this, be sure that he starts at the left and follows the parts sequentially.

If you care to do so, make enough of each so that each letter-shape can be reconstructed. The six pieces you have are sufficient for matching each separate part of each letter. Start with the *a* shape. Have the child place a short straight line and circle on top of their counterparts. Remind him of the left and right positions. Be sure that he places each part consecutively, starting at the left. Use the same procedure for each letter-shape. The *f* will have three parts—a long straight line, a short straight line and a small curved line. Repeat as he matches them. "Long straight line—be sure it's above the shelf; curved line, to the right facing down; short straight line—across the tall line, below the curve."

The *m* has five parts, but only two different matching lines, which will have to be put down, picked up, put down and so on. For instance, the short curved line must be turned over in order to use it for both the *f* and *g*.

If you save the materials, you can perform this activity many times before the child starts to school. The tracing of the shapes will be very effective later, when he is learning to spell words.

Supplementary Activities   Look through books or magazines and have the child point out the shapes he has learned. Lower-case letters are not found in some books, so be careful not to confuse the child by saying the names as you look at the printed letters; just have him tell you whether lines and curves are on the right or left, above or below a certain place.

Make the shapes of the lower-case letters on paper or on a blackboard for him to copy.

Make rows of the shapes of the letters on paper, preferably on a rough paper towel, and have him trace them in the proper direction.

Check Test   Go over the questions in the pretest again.

PART II

GETTING READY TO READ

INTRODUCTION

Since an ability to read plays such a vitally important part in a child's process of learning, as well as in the full enjoyment of the world around him, he must be given every opportunity to learn to read, not merely adequately, but skillfully.

The exercises and activities in Part I of this over-all program have been designed to provide cabled sensory perception. If this training has been completely absorbed, then your child is firmly launched on the road to expert, enjoyable reading.

But this is not the entire picture.

You, as a parent, must supplement this earlier training with an appreciation of broader areas of learning that will contribute to good reading habits.

To be completely at home with the printed word, your child must have a solid grounding in abstract symbols. He must have the self-discipline that will permit him to make use of everything he has learned up to this point.

He must be able to give his undivided attention to what he hears, as well as be able to show interest in it.

If he can listen to and enjoy short nursery rhymes, poems, songs, and other word activities, and later extend his span of attention so that he can sit beside you quietly as you read simple stories to him or as you turn the pages of picture books, he already will have progressed a long way.

When he has accomplished that much, you can add other steps. Show him that the words in sentences start at the left; as you read to him, have him move his eyes to follow your finger across the page. Explain that these things are what he must know and do when he starts to read for himself. Demonstrate with your finger how his eyes must go diagonally back to the left to start with the second line of symbols. This will help him to understand the reading pattern of eye movement and also give him good visual training.

Recognition of word symbols is not important at this time, as a child's ability to focus his eyes does not develop until he is about six years old. In many children's books, the words and pictures are large enough so that you can point out likes and differences in size and shape. If a child is attentive and not too restless, he may be able to note the configuration of the beginnings and endings of some words.

As the child increases his ability to move his eyes across the page, he becomes ready for the next step. You can gradually begin to slide your finger along beneath entire phrases, to give him a sense of smoothness in what he hears and in the movement he sees as he follows with his eyes. He may be interested in making the same sort of movement pattern with his own finger, thus adding his sense of touch to that of sound and sight.

Another important part of learning to read skillfully can be put into practice at this time. Recognition of sequence should be developed. You could stop, while reading a story, and say: "Now, let's see; this happened, then this. What do you suppose will happen next?"

In this way, you will be giving the child practical training in comprehension as well as encouraging the motivating, creative force of anticipation. Allow him as much of this type of participation as his interest and ability permit.

All this preparation is as much a part of reading as are the names, shapes, and sounds of the letters. The activities that follow are not the beginning or the end of reading; instead, they are fresh approaches that may be used to fill in the gaps that are sometimes evident in a child's learning pattern. These gaps may be due to his lack of readiness when certain of these steps were presented to him earlier in your home training, or at school.

The activities are not designed as a complete reading course, to be followed arbitrarily or exclusively. They are presented as suggestions to help you to open still wider for your child the magic door of reading.

It must also be remembered right from the start that the activities so commonplace to you will appear as almost impenetrable mysteries for your child. Repetition that may seem boring to you at first will become infinitely less so as your child performs each task, slowly, painstakingly, step by step.

Some of the activities will take longer to complete than others, but probably nothing in this planned program for your child is as important to his future as these basic fundamentals of the reading process.

Chapter 13

THE NAMES OF
THE LETTERS

In learning the names of the letters, the child will have a chance to make use of his perception skills, particularly his knowledge of position, direction, shape, and size. He will be able to use his sense of what comes first and what should come next to learn the sequence of the letters as they appear in the alphabet.

You will be given a pattern for showing your child how to learn one fundamental element of the communication skills; the alphabet, the names and shapes of the letters and how to make them. You will be able to show him how words, the tools of oral and written expression of ideas, are made up of these letters.

Some children learn best by seeing the whole pattern first and then breaking it down into its component parts; some build up from the basic facts to make the complete pattern; others learn by various methods somewhere between these two extremes. Although each child has his own individual pattern, each will profit by cabling his sense—by using his eyes, ears, and hands in unison as he learns the letters. Since many of the sounds are included in the names, the letters can play an important part in a child's learning to spell and to read.

AIMS

1. To learn to say the names of the letters.
2. To learn the four divisions of the dictionary.
3. To note the similarities and differences in the lower-case letters and in the capitals.
4. To use the eyes, ears, and hands in unison.
5. To perfect the memory.

PRETEST

1. Does the child know any of the 26 letters by sight?
2. Can he point out those that are made with complete circles?
3. Can he tell which circles are on the left of the lines? The right?
4. Can he point to those that have parts of circles?
5. Can he point to the short, straight, up-and-down lines?
6. Can he point to the slanted lines?
7. Can he point to those that go below and above the lines? Those that are made completely within the middle space?

Below you will see pictured the entire alphabet in manuscript. Both capitals and lower-case letters are divided into the four groups as they appear in the four quarters of the dictionary. If the child becomes familiar with these groups, he will find dictionary use easier later on.

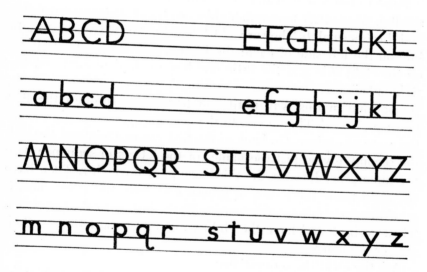

In the middle of a dictionary he can find words beginning with the letter *m*. In the first quarter are those words beginning with *a, b, c* and *d*.

One fourth of all words are in this first group. The other divisions are made according to the number of words beginning with letters in the groups.

In learning the alphabet, it is well to maintain these same divisions as a child can absorb a small block of information before going on to another. Using this method a child will also learn where to locate words in a dictionary.

Do not fail to call his attention to the lines, which help point out how the letters would look if they were made on lined paper. This will establish the comparative sizes of the letters as well as their configuration within the middle space and above and below it.

Activities   The alphabet is a good starting place for orderly sequential learning. Have the child move his eyes back and forth as he examines the letters. Point out that there are four groups. Say something like this: "These are the letters of the alphabet. See, there are two of each, one above the other. The bigger ones are called capitals and they are used to begin important words, like your name and mine."

Point to the first two and say: "This is a capital *A* and this is a small *a*. They don't look much alike, do they? This is a capital *B* and this is a small *b*. They are a little more alike. There is a straight line on the left side of each; the big one has two parts-of-circles on the right side and the little one has a complete circle on the right side."

Continue in this way until you have gone through the first group, *a*, *b*, *c*, *d*. Then go on to the next group, *e* through *l*, using the same procedure. Go back to the first group again and through the second, giving just the names of the letters in sequence. Use the same procedure for the third group, *m* through *r*. Then have the child name the letters in groups one, two, and three. This is good memory training. Continue with the last groups, *s* through *z*. Then go back and have the child name all of the letters in their proper sequence.

Ask the child these questions:

1. What is the name of the first letter of the alphabet? The last?
2. What is the last letter in the first group?
3. What are the first and last letters in each group?

If he cannot answer these questions by naming the letters, let him point to them. He will have plenty of time to review and learn the names as time goes on. Do the same with the following questions by having him name as many of the letters as he can and pointing to the others.

1. Which of the capitals are made with complete circles? (O, Q)

2. Which of the small letters are made with complete circles? (a, b, d, g, o, p, q)

3. Which of the small letters look something like the capitals? (c, i, j, k, p, s, t, u, v, x, y, z)

4. How is the small b like the capital B?

5. Which small letters are made above the middle space? (b, d, f, h, k, l, t)

6. Which small letters are made below the middle space? (g, j, p, q, y)

7. Which small letters have dots over them? (i, j)

8. Which capital letters have straight lines from left to right? (A, E, F, L, T)

9. Which small letters have slanted lines? (k, v, w, x, y, z)

10. Which small letters are made within the middle space? (a, c, e, i, m, n, o, r, s, u, v, w, x, z)

Chapter 14

THE LINES USED
TO MAKE THE LETTERS

Learning to make the strokes used in forming the letters is the child's next step. First of all, he must be taught that they are all straight lines, complete circles, or parts of circles. It is profitable to give some practice in making each smoothly, starting at the right place, moving in the right direction and stopping again at the right place. After the child has become adept at making the lines, he can then proceed to learn how to put them together and space them.

He should trace each line in the illustration above with his finger, then try to make it on unlined paper, then put it in its proper position on the lined paper.

What you say in giving directions is optional; some suggestions are given. In making up your own words, remember that great detail and repetition is often necessary if a child is to learn things correctly. Give exact and specific directions each time until you are sure the child can "do it all by himself."

Before the lined paper is brought into use, call attention to the three spaces. Be sure that the child knows which is the middle space, which is the upper, and which is the lower; he should know what is meant by the top line, the bottom line and the two middle lines; which is left, which is right; which is up, which is down. He must be able to distinguish between curved and straight lines and tell which lines slant and which go straight across. He must have concepts of *above* and *below, before* and *after, short* and *long, larger* and *smaller.*

Lined paper of the type needed may be purchased, but it is not too difficult to line some yourself with the help of a ruler. Make four horizontal lines across a sheet of paper, about a half-inch apart; leave about an inch before starting to make the next four lines. The size of the spaces may be larger or smaller in your own judgment of whichever size seems best for your child.

Large-sized primary pencils are usually used by beginners, but it seems reasonable to suppose that any pencil that is easy for a child to grasp would be satisfactory.

AIMS

1. To make use of the perception skills.
2. To insure adeptness in the use of the small hand muscles.
3. To listen to and follow directions.
4. To coordinate the use of the eyes, the ears and the hands.
5. To learn to make the lines needed for constructing letters.

MATERIALS NEEDED

1. Plain white paper.
2. Paper lined as described.
3. Picture of a child's hand holding a pencil, accompanying this chapter.
4. Lines with stars, accompanying this chapter.

Activities Place the plain paper straight in front of the child. Have him hold his pencil as shown in the picture. The wrist and forearm should rest lightly on the table and the fingers should slide along easily as he writes. The pencil should be held so lightly that it can be pulled out of his hand with little effort. If the child uses his left hand, the pencil can be held in the same general way. He should move his whole arm, rather than just the fingers.

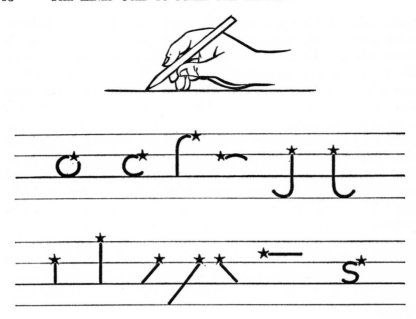

After the child has learned how to place his paper and hold his pencil, he can put them aside as he looks at the illustrations of the starred lines.

Say something like this: "Look at the circle and put your finger on the star. Move your finger around to the left, follow the line around, go up and close the circle. Do it again; now again. Now have your paper ready. Take your pencil and make some circles. Start where the star would be, go around, try to make it round, and close it up."

If necessary, place a star or dot to show him where to begin. After he knows where to start and how to move, let him make several circles on the paper. When he can do this pretty well, give him the lined paper and see if he can make some circles within the middle space. This may take quite a bit of practice—and paper —but do not let him feel discouraged; he cannot be expected to do it perfectly right away.

Have him make a circle within the middle space, then lay down two of the fingers of his other hand beside it and make another one beyond them. This will teach him how to space letters. Have him make a row of circles across the page. He should move his hand across the page as he makes them and move the paper up when he starts the next row.

Proceed in the same way with the c shape. Say something like this: "Start at the top star, move your finger around to the left, follow the line around the part of a circle and stop at the other star."

After he has traced the shape with his finger, have him practice on the unlined paper, then make some on the lined paper. He should space some of these also.

The next is a tall line with a curve at the top. Have the child trace it with his finger, starting at the star, curving around to the left and moving down in a straight line. Say something like this: "This looks like a cane. The top curves, but the rest is straight."

After the child has practiced on the unlined paper, give him the lined paper and say: "There are three spaces here; start almost at the top of the top space, go around the curve and straight down to the bottom of the middle space. Use your finger to space the canes, and make a row of them across the page."

The next curved line goes to the right and is made at the top of the middle space. Be sure that he traces with his finger the one in the illustration before he makes any on his paper.

The next line, an upside down cane, starts at the top of the middle space and goes on down into the lower space; the little tail curves to the left. The next line is straight but the tail curls to the right.

The short vertical line must be made within the middle space; the long one must start just below the top line and go straight down to the bottom of the lower space.

The first slanted line goes to the left within the middle space, the next goes to the left, down through two spaces. The last slanted line goes to the right, within the middle space.

The short, horizontal cross-line is made toward the right; where it is made is not important at this time.

Be sure that the child traces each pictured line with his finger before he tries to make it with his pencil.

For the s shape, say something like this: "Put your finger on the top star. Go to the left, then follow the curve around to the right, then go around and back to the left, to the other star. Trace it over and over again."

Have him look carefully at the *s* shape and say: "If you could turn the bottom part upside down and make it face the other way, it would fit exactly on the top part. Now, you try to make some with your pencil that would fit that way, too." This is good training for spatial relationship.

After he has made several *s* shapes on the unlined paper, let him try to make some on the lined paper within the middle space. Have him space the shapes on the lined paper. Be sure that he learns to go in the right direction to make the *s* shape.

The letter *s* often causes difficulty, especially with children who have a tendency toward reversal. If your child seems to be having trouble, let him practice as long as necessary—until he makes it correctly every time.

As a test, have him make a row of each of the thirteen parts he has learned to make. Perhaps one of each kind will be enough.

Watch the position of the child's paper and the way he holds his pencil. Good habits established early will help him to concentrate on other things later.

An excellent device for this type of training is a rough paper towel. Make the shapes of the letters on the towel and have the child trace them with his sensitive fingertips. Use the same method later, when he is making the letters and also when he begins to learn how to spell words.

These practices will prepare the child for the next steps, which will be concerned with how to make the letters.

Chapter 15

HOW TO MAKE
THE LETTERS

The most advantageous time to help a child learn the skills concerned with abstract symbols is during the period when his physical ability and his interest are ready.

The small muscles of his hands must be strong enough to hold a pencil steady without tiring easily; his eyes must function properly and be capable of coordinating with his hands to insure correct spatial relationships.

He must be able to connect the name of the symbol with its shape.

You can discover these things by "trying him out." Enthusiasm and repetition are the keys to learning the names of the letters and how to make them. Enthusiasm stems from a desire to break the secret code of words and numbers. If you offer a sequential, orderly, yet entertaining pattern for learning, which of necessity includes repetition, a child usually will respond.

Although your child may not yet *really* know the four quarters of the alphabet, as presented previously, or be able to say the whole alphabet in sequence, you need not be concerned. Indeed, it would be surprising if he had learned all this perfectly in such a short time. The classifications of letters given next and those appearing later will enable him to establish the names and, therefore, some of the sounds, as well as help him to recognize and make the shapes. He will also establish many habits necessary to skillful reading.

AIMS

1. To follow directions.
2. To use the hands with ease.
3. To practice perception skills.
4. To note similarities and differences.
5. To analyze and make logical choices.
6. To follow sequence patterns.
7. To utilize repetition as a means of memorizing.
8. To practice recall.
9. To learn to make the letters, grouped according to size and special relationship. (Since there is more than one way to make *some* of the letters, you may wish to check with your child's teacher before starting this segment of the training.)

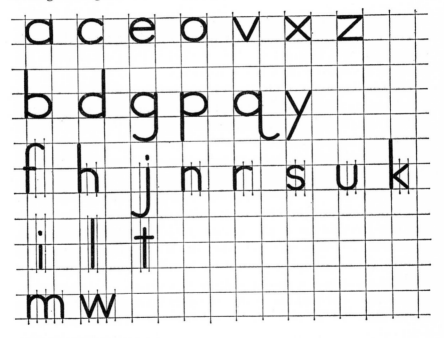

MATERIALS NEEDED

1. Illustrations of letters made within squares, accompanying this chapter.
2. Paper squared similarly for use by the child. Have several sheets, for the child may wish to make more letters. Graph paper with large squares may be purchased.
3. Pencil.

Activities The first lesson is concerned with the shape and size of the letters *a*, *c*, *e*, *o*, *v*, *x*, and *z*. All these are made within the confines of squares of equal size.

Have the child look at the illustrations showing this group of letters. Say something like this: "Here are some letters. Is this the whole alphabet? No. Are they in the order of the alphabet? No. How are they alike? They are all made inside squares, the middle squares. How are they different? Some are round and some are made with straight lines.

"Tell me the name of the first letter. Yes, it is *a*. Put your finger on the right side of the top of the square that contains the *a*. Remember where the star was, on the pattern of the circle? Start there and trace the circle with your finger. Go back around, close it up, keep inside the square. Now lift your finger, put it at the top of the line on the right, and go down. That's how you make an *a*. It's not hard, is it?

"Now, here's a pencil and here is a paper with squares the right size for the letters. Make an *a* in the middle square of the first line. Start where the star would be, go back around and close the circle. Lift the pencil and start at the top of the right side of the square, go down to the bottom of the square. Good, you've made an *a*. Go right on, make an *a* in every other square of that line; that way, they won't be crowded.

"Now, let's make the next letter that fills a square. What is it? Yes, a *c*. Put your finger up where it begins, go back around and up a little, then stop. That is how a *c* is made. Take your pencil and make a *c* on your paper in the second line of middle squares. That leaves two spaces, two squares, between the *a* and *c*. Start near the top, go around and up, not all the way—stop before you close the circle—that's right. Now make a whole row of *c*'s.

"What is the next letter? It's an *e*. Put your finger on the left end of the straight line, go straight across; trace it with your finger. Go up and around, and finish it just as you did the *c*. Trace it again with your finger. Now make a row of *e*'s in the next middle row of squares.

"The next letter in a square is the *o*. You can do that easily. Trace it with your finger; start at the top, go back around and close it. Make a row on your paper, in the next row of middle squares."

Continue with the next letter.

"What is this? Yes, a *v*. Put your finger at the middle point of the bottom line of that square. That is where the two slanted lines meet, at the bottom of the *v*. Where does the first line start? That's right, at the top left hand corner. Trace the line with your finger. Slant down toward the right, to the middle of the bottom line. Pick up your finger and start at the top of the other slanted line, go down toward the left and meet the other line. Good. Now, make a row of *v*'s in the next middle row of squares.

"Now, we'll make an *x*. It's easy too. Put your finger at the left top corner of the square, move it down across to the right hand corner at the bottom. Pick up your finger, put it at the top at the right hand corner, now down to the left hand corner at the bottom. That's the way you make an *x*. Make a line of *x*'s on your paper now.

"We're ready for the last letter of this group. What is it? Yes, a *z*. That's the last letter of the alphabet, too, isn't it? Put your finger on the left top corner of the square and go along the top line to the right, go down to the left hand corner at the bottom— that part is like the *x*—now straight across to the right again, along the bottom line. Now, make a row of *z*'s. Start at the left, go across, zip down, then go right again; be careful, stop right at the corner. Now let's see if you can make a line of all the letters you have just learned."

The next group of letters includes *b*, *d*, *g*, *p*, *q* and *y*. This is an appropriate time to lay heavy stress on likes and differences in the areas of left and right, above and below, before and after. Much of reading ability depends upon these concepts, and for beginners, the similarity in configuration of *b* and *d*, *g*, and *p* often causes trouble.

If there is any confusion in learning to make these letters, concentrate on one at a time. Another suggestion is to find ways of strengthening the concepts of position. If these problems are straightened out now, the child can analyze the parts of the letters for himself, and always remember that the line always comes first in a *b* and always comes last in a *d*. He can anticipate what comes next and start using the all-important skill of making logical sequential choices.

The same type of squared paper should be used for making these letters.

Start with the letters that have circles in the middle squares and lines that go up into the top squares. They are alike in the shape of their parts, but different in placement, position, and sequence.

Say something like this: "Show me the letters that have circles and lines that go up. Yes, the *b* and the *d*. Show me the letters that use up the whole square but have lines in the squares below also. Yes, the *g*, *p*, *q*, and *y*.

"Trace the letter *b* with your finger. It comes before the *d*. The line comes before the circle. Put your finger at the top of the long line, in the upper square at the left. Go down, down, lift your finger and trace the circle at the right. Be sure to close the circle. Do it again. Here is your paper; make a *b*. Start in the top square, go down, down, make the circle; skip a square and make another one. Good. Now make a row of *b*'s."

Give the child instructions as long as he seems to need them, but let him try to do it by himself as soon as possible, so his initiative will not be stifled.

Continue: "Can you tell me which comes first in the *d*, the circle or the line? Right, the circle. Trace the *d* with your finger. Start at the top right corner of the middle square, go back toward the left and around to make a circle. Lift your finger, put it at the right upper corner of the top square, go straight down, down to the bottom of the middle circle. Trace it again. Now make a *d* on your paper. See how it is different from the *b*; the line on the *b* comes *before* the circle. Make a row of *d*'s on your paper. Be sure that you keep the circle inside the square; it just barely touches the sides of the square as it goes around."

For the sake of strengthening his recall, have the child make *b*, then *d*. Mix the sequence to see if he remembers which is which.

The remainder of this group of letters have parts that go down into the lower square. Use the same procedure; have the child trace them with his finger, then make them on his own paper.

Follow the alphabetical order in which they are presented—first the g, then the p, q, and y.

Say something like this: "Make the circle first for the g; start the line at the top right-hand corner of the middle square and go down, down into the lower square—not all the way, because you have to make a little curled tail, just a little curve to the left. Don't lift your finger to make the tail, go right around. Make a row of g's.

"Which comes first in the p? Yes, the line. Go down, down, pick up your finger, make the circle and you've made a p. Make a line of p's on your paper.

"Next is the q. This letter uses the middle square and has a line below, just as the g and p have. There is something different about this letter, though. It's like the g because the circle comes first, but the little tail is different. It goes in the other direction. Go around to make the circle, go down, down to make the line—not all the way—go a little way around to the right to make the tail. That's the way to make a q. The g goes around to the left, the q goes around to the right. Now let's make a row of q's."

Be sure that the child is leaving squares above and below the middle squares, as he makes the letters; otherwise the terms *top*, *middle* and *bottom* will have no significance to him.

Continue: "The last letter in this group is easy to make. The top part is just like the v. Start at the top, left hand corner, slant down toward the right to the middle of the bottom line of the square; lift your finger (or pencil), slant down to meet that line, then go down, slanting to the lower left corner of the bottom square. That's the way you make a y. Now make a row of y's."

Ask the child to make the letters g, p, q, and y in a row. Have him make all the letters he has learned so far—a, c, e, o, v, x, z, b, d, g, p, q, and y.

The last two groups of letters were those that are made within a whole square of the middle space, with lines going above and below. The next group are those that are made in only two parts— two thirds—of the middle square. The paper used for these letters should have the squares divided vertically into thirds, as shown in the illustration. This lesson is very valuable, as it shows new patterns that are different but still somewhat like those already followed. The child will need to apply his knowledge of the basic facts already learned to new problems. This experience, in effect, will parallel many situations he will face in the future.

Have the child look at the illustrations of the letters *f, h, k, j, n, r, u,* and *s.*

Say something like this: "Are these letters made within whole squares? No, they don't fill the whole squares, just part of the squares. They are made within two parts, two thirds of the squares. The *f, h,* and *k* go up into the top squares; the *j* goes down into the lower square; the *n, r,* and *u* are made in two parts of the middle square.

"What is the first letter in this group? Yes, the *f.* We'll start with the *f.* Remember the cane you learned to make? The *f* is made with a cane. Trace it with your finger. Start at the right, near the top of the upper square, not all the way up. Curve back toward the left side of the square, go down to the bottom of the square, on down to the bottom of the middle square. Pick up your finger and cross the *f.* Start at the left, go toward the right along the top of the middle square.

"Make an *f* on your paper. I'll put some dots to show you where to start and end the *f;* I'll put two more dots here, and here, to show you where to cross it. Make a line of *f*'s.

"Now we're ready to trace the *h.* Start on the left side of the upper square. Put your finger at the top of the square, go straight down, down to the bottom of the middle square. Lift your finger and place it a little way down from the top of the left side of the middle square. Go up over the hump, through two parts, then straight down to the bottom of that square. You've traced the *h.* Now we'll make one. Remember, it does not fill a whole square. Start on the left side of the upper square, at the top, and go down, down. Pick up your pencil, put it just below the top of the middle square on the line you just made, go around to the right, make a hump through two parts and go down to the bottom of the middle square, straight down. Make a line of *h*'s.

"Start at the top of the left side of the middle square to trace the next letter, *j.* Go down, not quite to the bottom of the lower square, curve around to the left. Remember how you made the tail on the *g?* Make the curve go through two parts of the square.

Now lift your finger and put it on the dot, just above the *j,* in the upper square. Trace the *j* again. Make one on your paper. Good, now make a row of them in the middle row of squares. Remember, in every other square.

"What is the next letter? A *k;* trace it. Put your finger at the top of the upper square in the left-hand corner. Go down, down to the bottom of the middle square. Slant down to the line you just made, to the center of the left side of the middle square. Start there and slant down toward the right until you come to the bottom of the middle square. That's the way you make a *k.* Trace it again. Make one on your paper. Start at the left, at the top of the upper space; go down to the bottom of the middle square; then go over two parts to the top of the middle square; slant to the left, then down again to the right. Make a row of *k*'s.

"Look at the next letter, *n.* Is it anything like the *h?* Yes, it takes only two parts of the square to make it and it has a hump. Start at the left-hand top of the middle square; go down to the bottom of the middle square; pick up your finger and put it just below the top of the middle square at the left side where you made the first short line. Now go around the curve of the hump, just two parts over, and straight down to the bottom of the middle square. Good, now you make one. I'll put dots where they will help you to know where to start and end the line, where to start and end the hump. Stop at the bottom of the square. Now let's make a row of *n*'s in the middle row of squares."

If the child needs more help, place more dots for the rest of the *n*'s.

Now say: "Trace the *r* next. Start at the top left corner of the middle square. Move your finger down to the bottom of that square. Pick up your finger and put it just a little below the top of the line you have made. Curve around through two parts of the square but stop before going too far down—just a little way. Trace the *r* again. Make an *r* now with your pencil. Start at the top of the square, go down, then make the curve. Make a row of *r*'s.

"What is the next letter? An *s.* That won't be hard, because you've already learned how to make those curves. It's made in two parts of the square. Trace it, starting at the right, curve up, back and around, touch the left side of the square, curve toward the right, through two parts again, now curve back again to the left and up to touch the left side of the square. Trace it again. Now make an *s* with your pencil. Remember, the top and bottom curves are the same size, only made in opposite directions. Move first toward the left, then around toward the right, then around toward the left. Make a line of *s*'s in the right place. Left, right, left. Keep the curves nice and round."

Continue: "Look at the *u*. Do you see anything funny about it? It's an *n* made upside down. If you could turn the *n* upside down, it would be a *u* and if you turned a *u* upside down it makes an *n*. The first part of the *n* is like a cup. Which comes first, the line or the cup? The cup, of course."

You may have to call attention to the cup's being a hump up-side down. It is important that the child notice these shapes in all positions, since much of early learning is seeing familiar patterns in different positions.

Go on to say: "Put your finger on the left top corner of the mid-dle square, go down and curve around to the right to make a cup; go through only two parts of the square. Pick up your finger, start at the top of the short straight line and go down to the bottom of the middle square. Trace the *u* again; go down and around, then pick up your finger and place it at the top of the line and move it down to the bottom of the square. Now make one with your pen-cil. I'll put some dots on the paper to help you. After that, make a line of *u*'s."

The letters *i*, *l*, and *t* are in a group by themselves because they are made in only one third of the squares. The *i* is made by draw-ing a straight line through the middle third of the middle square. The dot is made directly above, in the upper square. Have the child trace the letter and make a row on his paper.

The *t* starts just a little above the top of the middle square and extends down through the middle square. It is crossed by a hori-zontal line which follows the top of the middle square, through the middle third. Have the child trace the illustration and then make a row on his own paper.

The *l* starts at the center of the top of the upper square; a straight line is drawn down through the middle third of that square and on down to the bottom of the middle square. Have the child trace as before and then make a row of letters.

The *m* and *w* each fill one whole square and one part of another. Ask the child to look at the *m* and notice how it is like the *n*, except for having another hump which takes part of another square.

Then say something like this: "Start at the left top of the middle square. Go down to the bottom of that square. Start the hump as you did for the *n*; go around through two parts and down to the bottom of the square. That's an *n*. Now lift your finger again, go up almost to the top of the right side of that hump and make another one. Curve around through two more parts into the next square for one of them and go on straight down to the bottom of that square. That's an *m*. Trace it again. Now make an *m* on your paper. Be sure to go past two parts for the first hump and past two more parts for the next hump. Make a row of *m*'s on your paper. Remember to leave just part of a square between the *m*'s, the part left over."

Continue with the last letter. Say: "Look at the *w*. It looks more like a double *v* than a double *u*. The v-shapes are narrower than the *v*'s, though. Each one fills just one part of a square. Trace it. Start at the left top corner of the middle square, slant down through one part to the bottom line of the square; then slant up to the right, through the next part of the square, down to the right through another part, then up through a part of the next square. The *w* is as wide as an *m*. Make one on your paper, always toward the right, down, up, down, up. That's good. Now make a row of *w*'s. Space them as you did the *m*'s. Now, you've made all the letters of the alphabet in squares."

The child, by having analyzed and made the letters, will now be fairly familiar with them. You can now progress to making them on lines. The paper should be lined as shown in the illustration.

A quick lesson on the three classifications—between the two middle lines, between and above, and between and below—may be helpful.

Say something like this: "Remember, you made all of the letters that came within the middle square. Well, you've done so well at that I think you won't need the squares any more. We'll use just lines. First, make all the letters that come between the middle lines. Make an *a*. Remember to make it fat and round. Ready? Back around, close it and come straight down.

"Now a *c*. Start as you did for the *a*, but don't close it."

Continue with the *e, i, m, n, o, r, s, u, v, w, x,* and *z.* Give the child specific directions when he needs them. Use dots to indicate the shape when necessary. Have him use the middle and upper spaces for *b, d, f, h, k,* and *l* and the middle and lower spaces for *g, j, p, q,* and *y.*

Remember that at this age a child's muscles tire easily. It may take quite an amount of practice for him to learn the names, shapes, and placement of all the letters. You'll undoubtedly want to vary the activities to be sure the child knows them all. For instance, one day he could make the letters that come between the lines and another day the ones that come above and below.

a c e m n o r s u v w x z

b d f h k l t   g j p q y

A further step toward his formal education is to change the sequence by putting the letters into the four quarters of the alphabet —abcd, efghijkl, mnopqr, stuvwxyz. Before you know it, he will be able to write the entire alphabet in sequence and in the various classifications.

The capital letters are illustrated also. They all are made with straight lines, circles, or parts of circles. Have the child start at the top of each letter. Most of them begin on the left side; the *C, G, O, Q* and *S* start at the right and the lines curve toward the left. The cross-lines (horizontal lines) on the *E, F,* and *H* are usually made slightly above the center of the letters, and those on the *A* and *G,* a little below.

Chapter 16

CURSIVE WRITING

All schools do not use exactly the same methods for teaching either form of writing. If you are going to help your child learn how to write, perhaps you should check with his school to be sure that you are not in any way going against established procedure.

The transition from manuscript to cursive (sometimes called long-hand) should be smooth. Let the child look at the letters in both forms and compare them. He should note their likes and differences. The sequence given here should strengthen the points of variation and enable the child to straighten out possible difficulties.

Your child should use larger spaces if that helps him to write better, or if the teacher wishes him to do so. Often children learn to write more legibly and more neatly when they use small spaces.

The child should sit in a relaxed position directly in front of a desk or table and place the paper at a 45 degree angle. Ideally, he should rest his forearms on the muscle nearest the elbow and support his hand by the nails of his third and fourth fingers; he should keep his wrist free from the surface and hold his pencil lightly between the thumb and middle finger. The index finger should rest on top of the pencil. If the child can follow these instructions, he will find that writing will not tire him; his fingers will not become cramped, and he will be able to move his hand rhythmically, easily, and with the necessary speed. The paper can be moved up, as needed, so the arm muscle can remain comfortably on the desk or table.

First have the child make the letters that come between the two middle lines, as shown on page 113.

Emphasize the fact that these are the letters that come between those particular lines, so he will understand what you mean when you say "the top line" or "the bottom line."

Straight lines are slanted down toward the left in most of the letters of the alphabet. Tell the children that when you say "straight" you mean slanted straight down toward the left. If these lines are kept parallel, the writing will look neater and rhythmic movement will result.

It should also be noted that the letter *z* is the only one which does not appear in both groups.

a c e i m n o r s u v w x z

a c e i m n o r s u v w x z

Undoubtedly the greatest difficulty experienced by a child when first learning cursive writing is in the joining of the letters. This is a matter that will be taken up later and can be disregarded at this stage. Thus, the letters are written here as they would be at the beginning of words.

Say something like this: "What is the first letter? Yes, an *a*. It is made almost like the one you have learned to make. Start at the top, at the right, go around to the left, close the circle, then make a straight line down to the bottom line, then a curved line up to the top middle line.

"The *c* starts with a little dot, then go around to the left, just like the *a* only don't close it, curve slightly up to the top middle line.

"Now the *e*. Start at the bottom middle line, curve up to the top line, around to the left, make a loop and go straight down, then curve up again to the top line.

"Next the *i*. (Ask the child each time, of course, to tell you the letter.) Curve up, then start down on the same line; no loop, make a point, go straight down and curve up to the top line. Now, what goes over it, just like the other *i* you made? Right! A dot directly over the *i*, not too high.

"The *m*. How many humps have you been giving an *m*? Yes, two. This *m* has another one. Remember that it's different. Curve up to the top line so that you can go around to make a hump, then go straight down to the line, curve around to make another hump, straight down, up to make the third hump, then straight down and curve up to the top line.

"The *n*. How many humps? Two. It's different, too. You've been making only one. Curve up, around to make a hump, straight down, up again to make another hump, straight down, then curve up to the line.

"The *o*. Make a circle, just as you did before, only this time come down a tiny bit and make a curved line out to the right. See, this line does not come down to the line, it goes almost straight out. Remember that. The line on the *o* must never come down to the line; if it did, you would have an *a*.

"The *r*. It isn't much like the manuscript. Make a curved line up, go a bit above the line, down straight a little bit, then slant down a little to the right, then go straight down to the bottom line, then curve up to the top line." (Note that another type of *r* is taught in some schools. This is a hump, then straight up to make a point above the line, then down a little and out to the right as in an *o*. This method should be used if it applies to your child's school.)

"An *s* looks quite different from the other *s*. Curve up to the top, make a little point as you did for the *r*, then curve out and around to the first line you made, close it, then curve to the top line.

"The *u*. Curve up, straight down, make a cup by curving up again, straight down, then curve up to the top line. See how it is different from the *u* you made before.

"The *v*. This doesn't have a point like the other one. You curve up and around to make a hump, then you curve down and make a cup, then curve up to the top line, come down a little bit and go out, just as you did when you made an *o*. The line on the *v* does not come down to the bottom line, either.

"The *w*. Curve up, come straight down, curve up to make a cup, then straight down, curve up again to make another cup, then down a little and out, just as you did when you made an *o* and a *v*. This line must not come down to the bottom line, either.

"The *x* starts out like the *v;* curve up and around to make a hump, then a straight line down, and a curved line up to the top line. Now start at the top line and make a slanted line down toward the left to cross the other straight line in the middle. This is the first time you've had to take your pencil off the paper while writing a letter except when you dotted the *i*.

"Now we'll make the letters that come *above* the middle line."

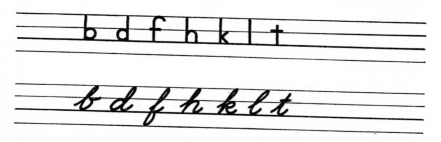

Have the child name these letters. Point out how the *f* comes both above and below the middle space. Tell him that *f* is the only letter that does this.

Then continue: "What is the name of the first letter in this group? Yes, a *b*. Notice that the loop is on the same side as the straight line on the manuscript *b*. Curve up, up to the very top line, curve around to the left, then straight down, down to the bottom middle line, curve up to the top middle line, down a little and a curved line out to the right, just as you did for the *o*, *v*, and *w*.

"The *d*. The circle is first, just as it is on the manuscript *d*. Make the circle, then go up, up almost to the very top line and back down around to the left to make a narrow loop, then curve up to the top middle line."

"The *f*. It's not much like the manuscript *f*, is it? Go up, just as you did for the first part of the *b*, around to the left, straight down, down, then down some more below the bottom middle line to the very bottom line; then go around to the right. Be sure to remember that you go around to the right. Curve all the way around and close the bottom loop at the bottom middle line, then curve out to the right and go up to the top middle line. Notice that there is a long straight line on the left side of the *f*.

"The *h* is a little like the manuscript *h*, but it has a loop instead of a straight line. Curve up, up, around to the left, straight down, down, to the bottom middle line, curve up and around to make a hump toward the right, straight down, and then make a curved line up to the top middle line.

"The *k*. Another loop, up, up around to the left, straight down, down, then go up as if you were making an *h*, only after the top part of the hump is made, go back toward the left, then straight down and curve up the top middle line.

"The *l* is still another loop. Go up, up, around to the left, straight down, down, then curve up to the top middle line. That's an easy letter to make.

"The *t*. Curve up, up, almost to the very top line, then straight down, down, no loop for the *t*; then curve up to the top middle line. Cross the *t* with a short line in the middle of the top space."

The rest of the letters are made with parts below the middle space. The loops on the *g, q, y,* and *z* are sometimes made a little longer than those on the *f, j* and *p*.

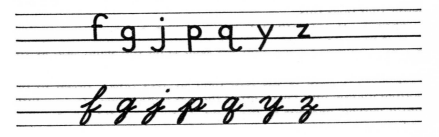

Continue: "What is the first letter in this group? It's another *f*. Well, that's one of the hardest letters to make, so we'll do it again. Go up, up, make a loop around to the left, straight down, down and down and a loop around to the right, close it, and make a curved line up to the top middle line.

"The *g* has a circle first, just like the manuscript letter. Make the circle to the left and around, close it, go straight down, down, around to the left to make a loop, then up, up, up and end at the top middle line.

"The *j*. Curve up to the top middle line, making a point as you go straight down, down, down, then curve around to the left to make a loop and go up, up, up to the top middle line. Dot the *j* just as you did the *i*.

"The *p*. The loop is first here, just as the straight line is on the manuscript letter. Curve up to the top middle line, then go straight down, down, down, go around to the left, make a narrow loop, curve around and up, up, up to the top middle line and around toward the right, down and all the way around to make a complete circle; close the circle, then go back down to the bottom middle line and curve up again to the top middle line.

"The *q*. Make a circle, just as you did for the *g*; also just as you did for a manuscript *q*. Then go straight down, down, down and curve around to the right, as you did for the *f*, to the right and make a loop around and up, up to the bottom middle line, then curve out toward the right and up to the top middle line.

"The *y*. Go up and around as you did to make a *v*, to the top middle line, make a hump, then go straight down to the bottom middle line, curve up to the top middle line, then go straight down —there'll be a point on top—go down, down, around to the left, to make a loop, then up, up to the top middle line.

"The *z*. Look, it's much different from the manuscript *z*. That is made between the middle lines and this one goes below the middle space. Make a hump within the middle space, as if you were starting an *m*. Go around to the right, straight down to the bottom middle line, then go up and around to the left to make a little loop, go around, then straight down, down, then around to the left to make a loop as you did for the *y* and curve up, up to the top middle line. This is the last of the letters.

"Now you'll have to learn to join some of them together. The letters *a*, *c*, *d*, *g*, and *o* will have to be given little curved lines at the beginning for joining them with other letters and some of the others will have to have a little taken off the ends so the connection will be smooth. The hardest letters to join will be the *b*, *o*, *v* and *w*. The letters you make after these cannot start at the bottom middle line; they will have to start up there, almost at the top middle line."

The letters given in this group are those that are most commonly joined. They will call the child's attention to the usual vowel and consonant combinations used in the formation of words. Even without knowing the facts, he will become visually aware of which letters have a natural relationship. He will meet the same ones later when learning the sounds.

Have the child write and join these letters:

ab, ac, ad, ae, af, ag, ah, ai, aj, ak, al, am, an, ao, ap, aq, ar, as, at, au, av, aw, ax, ay, az

ba, be, bi, bo, bu, bl, br, bs, bt, by

ca, ce, ci, co, cu, ch, ck, cl, cr, cs

da, de, di, do, du, dr

eb, ec, ed, ee, ef, eg, eh, ei, ej, ek, el, em, en, eo, ep, eq, er, es, et, eu, ev, ew, ex, ey, ez

fa, fe, fi, fo, fu, ff, fl, fr, fs, ft

ga, ge, gi, go, gu, gg, gh, gl, gn, gr, gs, gy

ha, he, hi, ho, hs, ht

ia, ie, io, ic, id, if, ig, ik, il, im, in, ip, ir, is, it, iv, ix, iz

ja, je, ji, jo, ju

ka, ke, ki, ko, ku, kr

la, le, li, lo, lu, lb, ll, lr, ls, lt

ma, me, mi, mo, mu, mb, mm, mn, mp, ms, my

na, ne, ni, no, nu, nd, ng, nk, ns, nt, ny

oa, ob, oc, od, oe, of, og, oh, oi, ol, om, on, oo, op, or, os, ot, ou, ov, ow, ox, oy, oz

pa, pe, pi, po, pu, pl, pp, pr, ps, pt, py

qu

ra, re, ri, ro, ru, rf, rg, rh, rk, rl, rm, rn, rp, rr, ra, rt, ry

sa, se, si, so, su, sc, sh, sk, sl, sn, sp, sq, sr, ss, st, sw, sy

ta, te, ti, to, tu, th, tr, ts, tt, tw, ty

ub, ue, uc, ud, ui, uf, ug, ul, um, un, up, ur, us, ut, uu

va, ve, vi, vo, vu, vy

wa, we, wi, wo, wh, wn, ws

xa, xe, xt, xy

ya, ye, yi, yo, yd, yl, ym, yn, yr, ys, yt, yx

za, ze, zi, zo

Children as well as adults usually like to be distinctive in making capital letters. The patterns here show an easy way to make them until they have developed their own style.

The letters should rest on the same line as the small letters, the bottom middle line. They fill the two top spaces. It is better for the child to separate the letters from the rest of the words. Notice that many of the letters are with a downward stroke that necessitates this procedure.

ABCDEFGHIJKLMN

𝒶𝒷𝒸𝒹𝑒𝒻𝑔𝒽𝒾𝒿𝓀𝓁𝓂𝓃

OPQRSTUVWXYZ

𝒪𝒫𝒬𝑅𝒮𝒯𝒰𝒱𝒲𝒳𝒴𝒵

Call attention to the first lines of H, F, M, N, U, W, X, and Y. They are all alike, so that line can be practiced several times.

For better-looking capitals, the top portion of the G, H, I, J, K, Y, and Z should be larger than the bottom part. Call special attention to the U and V. Children often leave off the downward stroke of the U, due of course to the way they have made the manuscript capital.

The J, Y, and Z are the only letters that go below the bottom middle line.

The only capitals not made with one complete unbroken movement are the F, H, K, T, and X. All movements begins at the top except for the I, J, L, P, R, and S.

The upward sweep of the P, F, and R are optional.

Be sure that the child starts the I and J at the bottom middle line, swings around toward the left, then toward the right, down, and then finishes them according to the pattern.

Have the child make all the small letters and capitals in alphabetical sequence as a final practice step.

PART III

LETTERS AND THEIR SOUNDS

INTRODUCTION

Before a child can read with any degree of skill, he must have all the tools at his command.

As we have already discovered, he must be able to move his eyes in any direction with natural ease. He must also be able to recognize all the letters in the alphabet.

Now is the time when the child should learn the meanings of words and their uses. He must be able to recognize them by sight, by configuration, and by their separate component letters. These letters, of course, have both shapes and sounds. When the study of their shapes has been undertaken successfully, he should embark on a constructive program of learning the sounds of each individual letter.

In his study of the shapes of the letters and how to say their names, he is already a long way along the road to success, since the names include most of the sounds.

This section of the book, therefore, supplements his previous knowledge in a logical, sequential pattern.

As has been stressed so many times previously, these lessons are not designed to take the place of regular procedures followed in the classroom. They merely present a different mode of attack that should be of interest and value to any student of words as sequential groups of letters.

This material is presented in patterns. Thus, it is advantageous to absorb each section completely before going on to the next, particularly since each succeeding lesson will use much of what has been previously introduced.

Some children will learn faster than others. Some will merely say the words without comprehension. And since comprehension depends on the scope of a child's experience with the words he hears and the words he speaks, repetition is a vital part of the learning process.

The combinations of letters given in the following lessons are, for the most part, used to make combinations of sounds. It is hoped that the child will recognize many of them as words and be able to perform the supplementary activities. Any skills that he acquires by performing them will be valuable for spelling and vocabulary-building, as well as for reading and writing.

While learning the sounds, the student can use various means to make the process easier for him. He can hold his hands over his ears, as he is making the sounds; this may help him to distinguish the difference in the sounds he is voicing.

A sign depicting a skull-and-crossbones is pictured throughout these lessons. Explain to the child that this is a danger signal: when he sees it on a bottle or box, he knows the contents are dangerous. When he sees it placed over certain words he will know that it is a warning: he must watch out for trouble. The significance of the sign will soon become obvious to him.

The child will be given a chance to use his eyes, ears, hands, and voice, and to utilize his perception skills, as he notes sequence of position, direction, size, shape, and configuration, and matches his voice to the letters.

Beginners should not be expected to grasp the reasons for all the variations and exceptions appearing in the English language, but they may profit by hearing about some of them; older children usually find them very interesting. As time goes on, practice and familiarity will take care of many problems. Even exceptions fall into patterns, which will be shown later.

A word that does not conform to known patterns will be called a "learned word." When learning to spell such a word, the child should use the "paper towel technique." Write the word in rather large letters on a rough paper towel; have the child trace each letter with his sensitive finger tips, say its name, then pronounce the word. After using this form of training, involving touch and motion combined with sight, hearing, and voice, he will almost certainly remember how to write the word and how to spell it orally.

Take the towel away from him and have him make the letters in the air, or on the top of the desk with his finger. When words do not conform to sound-patterns, visual memory can also be brought into use. Have the child look at a word, then close his eyes. He may be able to see an "after-image," which makes a more lasting impression on the area of the brain that it reaches.

Have the beginner write the words in manuscript; any child who has begun cursive writing at school should use that.

AIMS

1. To practice perception skills and to cable the senses.
2. To use the vocal organs as directed and to match the voice to the sound.
3. To recognize sounds already heard in the names of the letters.
4. To recognize and distinguish between sounds heard and voiced.
5. To recognize similarities and differences in sounds and in shapes of letters.
6. To form correct judgments of right and wrong sounds.
7. To associate sounds with configuration, through hearing, seeing, feeling, and voicing.
8. To recall, imitate, and use sounds correctly.
9. To make speech-sounds by starting and stopping other voice sounds.
10. To interpret differences in pitch, loudness, volume, and intensity.
11. To make sounds with one or more pulses (beats) of the voice.
12. To find patterns and exceptions and learn them by rote, sorting, and perception sense.

MATERIALS NEEDED

1. The alphabet already used while learning to make the letters.
2. The groups of letters, as shown with each lesson.
3. Paper lined as before, with three spaces. If the child has learned to make the letters very well, he may not need to use lined paper; if he has not perfected his writing, this is another opportunity for him to acquire skill by more practice with and without the lines to guide him.
4. Pencil.

An additional aid to clarity in teaching and absorption of the material in this section of the book might be called, for the sake of identification, "configuration."

Lines have been drawn around these two words to emphasize the shape of the words themselves. A child can tell the likes and differences of words by noticing their configuration.

When appropriate, write the two words on the paper and have the child trace the shapes of the letters, saying the names, then pronouncing the words.

Be sure that he pays particular attention to the beginning of each word. Usually, if a child makes the right start in saying a word, he will be able to say the remainder.

Other words that might cause difficulty can be handled in this way when necessary.

Chapter 17

LEARNING THE LONG SOUNDS OF THE VOWELS

First make the shapes of the vowels on lined paper, and say something like this: "Put your finger on each letter and say its name. That's right. The vowels are *a, e, i, o,* and *u.* Say *vowel.* Now again, what are the names of the vowels?

"Vowels are very important, so important that there is one in every word. Sometimes there are more than one. You'll never see a word that does not have a vowel in it. The letter *y* is sometimes used instead of the vowel *i;* when this happens, *y* is a vowel, too. When a vowel says its own name, it is called a *long vowel.* What are the long vowel sounds? Yes, the same as their names, *a, e, i, o, u.* Make the long vowel sounds again; they are the same as the names."

Have the child say the names of the vowels several times, at the same time tracing the shapes with his finger. This will enable him to channel the sense of touch with those of seeing and hearing, thus strengthening the learning process.

Write the letters *w* and *y* on the paper. Say something like this: "Sometimes these letters are vowels. What are the names of these letters?"

Have him trace the letters with his finger, and say the names. Then continue: "When a *w* is used as a vowel, it does not say anything by itself. We'll learn more about that later. When the *y* is used as a vowel, sometimes it says nothing and sometimes it says the name of *i,* or makes another sound of *i.* What is the long sound of *y?* Yes, it is the name of *i.*"

127

Have the child make the letters *a, e, i, o, u,* and *y* on the paper and say their long sounds. He should do this several times.

Write these words on the paper: *I, by, my.*

Then say something like this: "Now, I want you to sound the long vowel in these words; just the vowels, never mind the other letters. What are the long sounds of these vowels? Look at the first vowel. It's a capital. What is the name of the letter? Yes, it's an *I,* and it stands for whoever is talking. The one who is talking is the most important at that time; that's why it is a *capital* letter. We have to pay attention to the person who is talking. None of the other letters are capitals."

Write the words: *be, he, me, we, go, ho, no, so.*

Say something like this: "Tell me all the long vowel sounds (*e, e, e, e; o, o, o, o*). Good. When vowels are on the ends of words like that, just one vowel in a word, the vowel has the long sound. Now let's say them again."

If the child wants you to tell him what the words are, it is all right to say them, but the long vowel sound is the important thing at this time. You could pick up a book or newspaper and have him see if he can find some vowels. This will help him establish the fact that there is one or more than one vowel in every word, even though these might not always say their own names.

Continue with something like this: "Vowels do not always say their own names. We'll learn other sounds later, but now we'll look at some more little words, where they *do* say their own names."

Write these words: *cane, date, ride, dine, code, cone, dune, rule.*

Continue: "See, these words each have two vowels. Whenever this happens, in little words like these, the first vowel is long and the last one, the one on the end, is silent. The first one says its own name and the last one doesn't say anything. Take your pencil and draw a straight line over the first vowel in each word."

Show the child how to do this and say: "That means that the vowel says its name. Say the name of the first vowel in each word (*a, a, e, i, i, o, o, u, u*); now take your pencil and draw a line right through the *e* on the end of each word. Start the line at the top and slant down through the letter toward the left. Don't make any sound for those vowels; they are put there just to make the first vowel say its own name. When you see an *e* on the end of a word, the first vowel is long."

Write these words: *day, may, say, way, gait, lead, read, see, lie, pie, tie, low, row, sow, due, hue.*

Ask the child to put a straight horizontal line over the first vowels and cross out the second vowels.

Continue: "These words each have two vowels, too. These vowels are together, but you sound them the same way; the first vowel says its own name, the next one doesn't say anything. See, the *w* and *y* are vowels here; they don't say anything. What do the vowels say? Yes, *a, a, a, a, a, e, e, e, i, i, i, o, o, o, u, u.*"

Supplementary Activities   Try to read to your child every day, preferably from the classics. The old nursery rhymes seem to hold a child's attention well, as do selections from Stevenson's *A Child's Garden of Verses,* and the children's poems of Longfellow, Whittier, and A. A. Milne. The standard fairy stories, fables, and Greek and Roman myths are always popular with children.

With beginners, move your finger across the page, under the words; have them follow with their eyes, then go back to the left of the page for the beginning of the next line, and continue smoothly from left to right. Remember that in reading, the eyes usually "take in" a phrase at a time, slipping rhythmically to the next.

Chapter 18

THE CONSONANTS WITH NAMES ENDING IN LONG VOWEL SOUNDS

Write the letters *b, c, d, g, p, t, v,* and *z* on your paper. Also write the letters *j, k,* and *q.*

Have the child look at these letters, put his finger on each, and say its name.

Then say something like this: "These letters are not vowels, they are consonants. Say the word *consonant*. These are only some of the consonants. They are alike in one way: Their names end with the name of a vowel. Say the names of all of those whose names end in a long *e* sound." He should say *be, ce, de, ge, pe, te, ve, ze.*

Then continue: "The sound of a consonant is never the same as its whole name. You fix your mouth to say the name, but you don't let the last part come out. Let's do that with the consonants ending in *e*. Trace the first letter with your finger, and start to say *be* —but don't finish it, don't say the *e*. Try again. Just the first part, remember." This is not easy. Have him do it over and over again until he can do it pretty well.

Write these letters on the paper: *ba, be, bi, bo, bu, by*. Tell the child that these are just sounds, not words. Tell him that sometimes the vowels have other sounds, but now he should say only the long sounds, because those are the ones he knows. Remember the *y* is *i*. Say something like this: "Make the sound of *b* with a long *a* sound after it. Make the sounds close together and use your voice only once."

Let him practice this several times, then go on to the next letter, *c*. When you combine the *c* sound with the vowel, explain, "There is something a little different about *c*. It has two sounds. When you put it before *e, i,* or *y,* it sounds just the way you learned it. When you put it before other letters it has a different sound. Say the letter *k*. That's right, *ka*. Sometimes the letter *c* has the same sound as the letter *k;* take off the long *a* sound and make the sound of *k*." Have him practice the sound of *k*.

Make these letters on paper: *ca, ce, ci, co, cu, cy*. Have him give their sounds. He should say *ka, ce, ci, ko, ku, cy*. Practice these sounds several times. Remind him that *y* has the same sound as *i*. Ask him, "When *c* is before *e, i,* or *y,* how does it sound? When *c* is before any other vowel how does it sound?"

Have the child learn and practice the sound of *d*, as he did the sound of *b*.

After he has learned the soft sound of *g*, tell him, "The letter *g* has two sounds, just as *c* has. Sometimes before *e, i,* and *y,* the sound of *g* is just they way you learned it."

Write the letters *ge, gi, gy*. Have him sound these, with the soft sound of *g*, then say, "Always before any other letter, and sometimes even before *e, i,* and *y,* the *g* has a different sound. Say the word *go*. Now start to say *go*, again, and take off the long *o* sound. That's right, you've made the other sound of *g*." Write the letters *ga, ge, gi, go, gu, gy;* have the child say, *ga, je, ji, go, gu, jy*. Use the long vowel sound only. The sounds of *c* and *g* should be practiced again with the soft vowel sounds after those have been learned.

The sounds of *p, t, v,* and *z* can be introduced and learned by the same method used for learning the sounds of *b* and *d*.

Point to the letters *j* and *k* on the paper. Say something like this: "What is the name of this letter? Yes, it is *j*. It ends with a long vowel sound; what is the vowel? It is *a*. Start to say the name of the consonant, and leave off the name of *a*. Now you have made the sound of *j*. It sounds like one of the sounds of another letter. Yes, like the soft sound of *g*."

Combine the letter *j* with the names of the vowels, *ja, je, ji, jo, ju*. Use the same procedure to teach the sound of *k*. Remind him that the sound of *k* is the same as one of the sounds of *c*.

Have the child trace the letter *q*, and say its name. Ask him to leave off the name of the letter *u*, and make the sound of *q*. Say, "It sounds just the same as *k* sounds, but when you see this letter in a word, it will always have a *u* after it; it will have a rather strange sound." The child has not learned the sound of *w* yet, so help him to make these sounds: *qua, que, qui, quo.*

Write the words below and let the child pronounce them. Tell him that these are not just sounds, they are words. He will probably be proud to be able to read some of them. He could write them, too: *be, go, I, by, bide, tide, bite, die, pie, eat, beat.*

Supplementary Activities   Saying one word at a time will not establish good reading technique. As soon as possible, the words should be put into some sequence that has meaning when read from left to right. So far, the long vowels and the first set of consonants have been presented. You can write a few short sentences and phrases that will accustom the child to sequential patterns of words.

He can try to read groups of words, moving his eyes from left to right, taking in one group at a time, then going on smoothly to the next. For example:

I bite.

I eat pie, day by day.

Chapter 19

THE SHORT VOWEL SOUNDS

The short sounds of the vowels are perhaps most difficult for a child to learn. They must be presented correctly. The child must be able to hear them accurately and give them back by voice so that they sound the same way.

If possible, show him how to fix his mouth as he makes the sounds. Show him where to place his tongue, and how to expel his breath so the sound starts and stops in a way that will give it its distinctive quality. Try each sound yourself, then explain what you did. The short *a* sound seems to come from the front of the throat, the short *e* sound from the front of the mouth, the short *i* sound from the top of the mouth, the short *o* sound from farther back in the throat, and the short *u* sound from still farther back. Much practice and repetition is needed. Have the child try holding his hands over his ears, to help him hear his own voice.

Have the child look at the pictures on this page and tell the name of what they represent—*apple, Eskimo, Indian, octopus,* and *umbrella.*

Ask him to say *apple*. Say it yourself and draw out the short *a* sound. Say something like this: "A-apple. Now drop off everything but the first sound, *a*. Say apple *a*, apple *a*, apple *a*." Be sure that he makes the short sound of *a*, tracing the shape of *a* as he makes the sound. Repeat this until he seems able to make the sound correctly. Watch his mouth to see where he places his tongue. Continue the same procedure with other *a* words, such as *add, after, attic, Allen.* Just say the words, do not write them.

Write these combinations of letters and have the child sound them: *ab, ad, ak, ap, at, az.* He should use his voice once only; be sure that he says *ab*, not *a-buh*. Have him trace the letters as he makes the sounds.

Continue with the other vowels and pictures in the same way. For *e*, you could follow the word *Eskimo* with the short *e* sound at the beginning of *end, ever, egg, Eddie, Ellen;* then proceed with *eb, ed, ek, ep, ez,* using one beat of the voice.

For the short *i* sound, after practicing with the word *Indian*, use *it, ink, if,* and *ill,* then continue with the sounds of *id, ik, ip, it, iv.* Tell the child that these are sounds, not words. (A short *y* has the same sound as short *i*.)

Follow the same routine with the short sound of *o*. After the word *octopus*, use such words as *object, odd, olive, otter,* then the sounds *ob, od, ok, op, ot.*

Continue with the short sound of *u*. After the word *umbrella*, use the words *up, under, ugly,* and *utter,* then the sounds *ub, ud, uk, up, ut, uv.*

Listen carefully and notice if the child is trying to avoid adding an *uh* sound.

Write these words: *bat, cat, pat, tat, vat, bet, pet, bed, Ted, ten, din, pin, dot, cot, pot, bun, dun, pun, pup.*

Let the child copy the words if he wishes to do so. Then continue: "These are little words, each containing one vowel. There is a consonant sound at the beginning and a consonant sound on the end of each word. When there is a consonant after one vowel and no *e* on the end of the word, the vowel has a short sound. You can say each of these words by using your voice once. The word is just as long as one beat of your heart. Put the first two fingers of your right hand on your left wrist. You can feel your pulse— the beat of your heart."

Show him how to do this, then continue, "When you say these words, make them just that long, like one beat of your heart. These short words have one syllable, one beat. You'll learn more about syllables, later. Now see if you can say the words."

Let the child learn to spell the word *bat*. Have him trace the shapes of the letters with his finger, saying the names of the letters as he does so, then the name of the word. This is one of the best techniques for learning to spell words, as the senses of seeing, hearing, and feeling combined with motion are cabled. It is particularly effective for words that do not conform to phonetic patterns.

Now look back at the letter *a* under the skull-and-crossbones. Say something like this, "Sometimes you will see that letter used as a word. When it is used as a word, it does not say its own name, and it does not have a short sound of *a*. It sounds like a short *u*. Use it as a word by itself. Say *a table, a chair, a boy*." Continue to practice with *a* used as a word before the names of objects.

Supplementary Activities Now that the short vowels have been taught, you can compose a number of other sentences and phrases. Let the child try to think of some, using only the first set of consonants.

Here are a few examples:

I bat.	*A bad cat.*
I bet.	*A big cat.*
I tap.	*A big bed.*
Pat a cat.	*A big bag.*

Chapter 20

CONSONANTS WITH NAMES BEGINNING WITH SOFT VOWEL SOUNDS

The names of the consonants *f, l, m, n, s,* and *x* all have the sound of short *e* before their own sounds. When the name of any of these is heard in a word, the letter always has an *e* before it, as in *left, tell, hem, men, best,* and *text.*

To learn the more usual sound of these consonants, the short *e* sound at the beginning must be dropped. These consonants have *closed* sounds. A child is not likely to say *fuh, luh, muh, nuh, suh.* However, this tendency must be watched for here. The *r* sound has a short *o* sound before it, but when its name is heard in words the spelling is *ar,* as in *car* and *park.*

Activities Write on your paper the letters *f, l, m, s, x,* and *r.*

Have the child look at the shapes of the letters, trace them with his finger, and say their names. Call attention to the short *e* sound at the beginning.

Say something like this: "Say the name of *f.* Start to say it again, but this time hold back the short *e* sound. The sound of the letter is just the last part. Keep the short *e* sound in your mouth, put your upper teeth on your lower lip and let only the last part come out." Show him how to do this. Be sure that you hear only the *f* sound, not *fuh.* The sound is not actually vocalized until it is followed by a vowel sound. Have him trace the letter as he makes the sound.

Write these letters and have the child sound them, first using the long vowel sounds, then the short sounds: *fa, fe, fi, fo, fu, fy; af, ef, if, of, uf.*

Remember, the *y* has the same sounds as *i.*

Follow the same procedure with the remainder of the short *e* consonants. For the *l,* have him put his tongue forward against the upper teeth and let the sound come out. For the *m,* have him bring his lips together and keep them together while he makes the sound. For the *n,* he should hold his tongue against the upper front teeth, but keep his lips apart.

IS

of

After he drops the short *e* sound from the name of *s,* his jaws should come almost together, and air should be expelled from between the teeth. Say to him: "You have made that sound before. Sometimes the *c* has that sound, when it is used before *e, i,* and *y.*

"Now look at the first word under the skull-and-crossbones. You must watch out for that word, because in that the *s* has the sound of *z.* Say the word." Have the child trace the letters in the word, saying their names, and then the name of the word.

When the short *e* sound is dropped from the name of the letter *x,* the sound of *ks* is left. When you have the child sound *x* with the vowels, let him omit the *x* before the vowels; sound only *ax, ex, ix, ox,* and *ux.*

When the child has finished all of the short *e* consonants, have him sound them again in sequence, then out of sequence to make sure he associates the correct sound with the shape of each letter. Have him look at the second word under the skull-and-crossbones, give it the sound of *uv,* trace the letters, say their names, then repeat the name of the word.

Continue with something like this, "Trace the shape of the letter *r* with your finger. What is the name of the letter? It starts with a short *o* sound, doesn't it? Say it again, but keep the short *o* sound back; let the rest come out. Move your tongue back a little; you sound something like a dog growling. Try it again."

Write these letters: *ra, re, ri, ro, ru.*

Practice with the long and short vowel sounds. Do not place the vowels before the *r* at this time; those sounds will be given later.

Write these words, and see if the child can sound them. Have him move his eyes up and down for these columns:

bad	*bed*	*bid*	*cot*	*bun*
dad	*fed*	*lid*	*dot*	*fun*
fad	*led*	*mid*	*got*	*gun*
gad	*red*	*rid*	*lot*	*run*

These words should be fun to say, as they rhyme. Words could be added, by going through the alphabet to find other consonants, already learned, that would make words if placed before and after vowels.

Say something like this: "Each of these words has one vowel with a consonant after it. That means that the vowel must be given a short sound. Each word has only one syllable—that is, you use just one beat of your voice."

Be sure that the child does not place an *uh* sound on the end of the consonants; call his attention to the sounds of *c* and *g*—all hard in these words.

Supplementary Activities   Most of the consonants have been sounded, so more sentences can be written. Henceforth, be sure that the child moves his eyes properly as he reads the sentences.

Whether you write the sentences or you have the child write them depends on his individual ability. Much of the supplementary work could be put off until the child is rested and eager to perform.

Examples:

I can see a cat. He is quite a big cat. He is big and fat.

I see Ted in a red cap. Ted can see me. Can Ted see Bill?

Bill ran a race, but Ted quit. I can run. You can run. Bill can run.

If the child asks about the question mark and periods, explain their use—for asking questions and telling things. A special point need not be made about his remembering these facts, but no doubt he will, if he sees them often enough.

Chapter **21**

THE CONSONANTS H, W AND Y

The consonants *h, w* and *y* are the only letters whose sounds are not included in their names. They are often used in unusual ways, some of which will be described here.

Write on your paper the letters *h, w,* and *y*. Then have the child look at the letters, say their names, and trace their shapes.

Say something like this: "Put your finger on the *h*. Trace it with your finger; say its name. Remember, *h* is a consonant. When you learned the name of the other consonants, you just said a part of their names. You can't do that with *h*. The name doesn't have the sound in it. I'll write the letters *h* and *o* on the paper. The *o* will be long. *H-o* says *ho*. You know, Santa Claus says, 'Ho-Ho.' You say *ho*. That's right, *ho*. Now say it again, and leave the long *o* sound off. Just open your mouth and let the sound come out. Trace the letter again, and make the sound."

Be sure that he tries to make just the *h* sound. Combine the *h* with vowels—*ha, he, hi, hu, hy*—and have him say them first with the long, then the short vowel sounds. Do not use any vowels before the letter *h*.

Write these words: *hat, hit, hot, hem, hen, hate, heat, home, huge.*

As the child pronounces these words, remind him that the first group contains words with short vowel sounds. The others have long vowels because there are two vowels; the second vowel makes the first one long. The first vowel is long, and the second vowel is silent.

Continue, "Put your finger on the *w*. Say its name. Trace it and say its name again. That's nothing like it sounds, either. I'll write the letters *w-e* on the paper. That says *we*. Say *we*. Now say it again, but leave off the long *e* sound. Sound just the first part. Make your lips sort of pucker, draw them back and let the sound come out. Now trace the letter *w* and make the sound."

Continue practice until the child can make the sound of *w*. Write these letters and have him sound them, first with the long vowel sounds, then with the short sounds: *wag, wig, win, wait, wail, wake, wane*. Have the child say the words, using just one beat of his voice for each. Have him decide which vowels should be short and which should be long.

Continue, "Put your finger on the *y*. Trace it, and say its name. Again, the name is nothing like the sound."

Write the letters *y-o* on the paper twice, *yo-yo*. Say, "You know what a yo-yo is. Say *yo-yo*. Now say *yo*. Leave off the long *o* sound, and you will have the sound of *y*. Try it again. Open your mouth, put your tongue back of your lower teeth, then bring it back and let the sound come out." Have him practice until he can make the sound of *y*, not *yuh*.

Write these letters: *ya, ye, yi, yo*. Have the child sound the *y*, first with the long vowel sounds, then with the short vowel sounds. Do not place *y* after the vowels, as this causes it to become a vowel.

Write these words: *yam, yet, yon, yale, yoke*.

Ask the child to decide which words have short vowels, and which have long vowels. If he has forgotten, repeat the reasons.

Look at the word under the skull-and-crossbones. It begins with the sound of *y*, but the first vowel is silent and the second is long. *Ou* has the sound of long *u* in this word. Have the child trace the letters, say their names, then pronounce the word *you*.

Say, "Make the sound of *y*, then the long sound of *u*. That's right, *y-o-u* spells *you*."

Supplementary Activities   See if the child can read some sentences like these:

I can run.
You can run.
He can run.
We can run.

I may win a race.
You may win a race.
He may win a race.

It may be early to teach the person and number of pronouns, but there is no harm in making a child familiar with the sequence followed in the above sentences; that is, the person speaking, the person spoken to, and the person spoken about.

He could also make sentences with different tenses.

I run.
I ran.
He will run.

Write these words on the paper: *hat, pan, din, bit, rob, rod.*

Say something like this: "These words have one syllable each. Each word has only one vowel, and it's followed by a consonant. That means that the vowel must be given a short sound. Say the words."

After the child has pronounced the words, continue with something like this: "I'll show you a trick. If you put a magic *e* on the end of those words, presto! You'll have a new word."

Have him place an *e* on the end of each word, or rewrite them with an *e* on the end, so that the words will be: *hate, pane, dine, bite, robe, rode.*

Continue, "Now what are the words? No more short vowels, just long, and the magic *e* is silent. Say the words."

Chapter 22

CONSONANT BLENDS
WITH L AND R

When two consonant sounds come together, particularly at the beginning of words and syllables, they are called blends.

A child may have some difficulty making them come out as one sound, so plenty of practice is needed. *B-l*, for instance, is not *buh-luh*, but *bl*. The letters in blends must never be sounded as two separate sounds, but as one sound. Doing this properly gives the child opportunities to listen, follow directions, and control his voice.

The letters *r* and *l* have sounds that blend well with a number of consonants. Notice that consonants other than those contained in the blends given here would not blend easily with *l* and *r*; for instance, *dl, hl, mr,* and *ml* would each require two sounds, not one. (*Sl* and *tr* are included in the next lesson.)

Write on your paper the blends *bl, cl, fl, gl, pl*. On the next line write the blends *br, cr, dr, fr, gr, pr*.

Have the child look at the blends *bl* and *br*. Say something like this: "Two consonants like these, together, are called a blend. A blend is something that is made of more than one thing. If you mix chocolate and milk together, what do you have? Yes, chocolate milk; not chocolate and milk separately, but chocolate milk. They blend together and make one thing. They become something different, but still have two things blended together to make one thing; chocolate and milk makes chocolate milk.

"Now put your finger on the *b*. What is the sound? That's right, *b*. Now put your finger on the *l*. What is that sound? That's right, *l*. Blend those two sounds and you will have *bl*—first the sound of

143

b, then right away, make the sound of *l.* Good." Be sure that the child uses his voice only once and says *bl,* not *buh-luh.*

Combine the sound of *bl* with the long vowel sounds, then the short sounds. Have him pronounce these words: *bled, bleed, blame.*

Proceed in the same way with *br* and, after practicing with the vowel sounds, use the words: *brim, brine, brake, brad, braid.*

Continue with all the *l* and *r* blends listed. Use the vowel sounds followed by some typical words.

These words could be sounded: *clan, clean, crate, cream, cry; drum, dry; flake, fled, fly; frame, free, fry; glad, glum; grade, gray, green; pled, pray, prim, pry.*

Have the child give the reasons for making the vowels long and short; remind him that *y* is the same as *i;* call his attention to the sound of *c* and *g* before the consonants.

Supplementary Activities   The child should be able to write and read more sentences now.

Examples:

I can not fly.
You can not fly.
He can not fly.
The plane can fly.
I will not cry.
You will not cry.
He will not cry.
No, we will not cry.

Watch the child's eye movement as he reads these sentences.

Chapter 23

CONSONANT BLENDS
WITH S AND T

The sound of the letter *s* blends with a number of other consonant sounds. The blends *sp, sk,* and *st* are sometimes used on the *ends* of words and syllables, as well as at the beginning.

The other consonant combinations used on the ends of words and syllables are different in that they can not be used at the beginning. For example, you can not start a word with the combinations *ck, nd, ng.* The sounds do not blend with each other, or with the vowels that may follow.

The ending combinations will not have to be learned as such. When two consonants, other than blends, come together, the child should merely be instructed to sound the letters, one after another, being careful not to insert any *uh* sounds. An *s* added to form the plural of a word should be handled in the same way.

The ending combinations most commonly used for one syllable words are as follows: *ck, nd, ng, nk, nt, pt, rb, rd, rk, rp, rt.*

The sounds of these can be practiced in words, as a separate lesson. Write on your paper the blends, *sc, sct, sk, sl, sp, spr, st, str, sn, sw.*

Have the child look at these *s* blends. Ask him to trace the shapes of the letters as he gives their names, then trace them again as he gives the sounds, trying to avoid any *uh* sounds. Have him sound them with the long and short sounds of the vowels. Remember that the *sc* blend has the sound of *s* when used before *e, i,* and *y.* It has the blended sound of *sk* otherwise. The three-letter blend *scr* always includes the sound of *k.*

The following words may be used for practice after the entire group has been learned: *scene, scan, scant, screen, skate, slat, slate, slant, spin, spot, spring, sting, string, state, snack, swing, hasp, clasp, fast, last.*

Now write and have the child look at the letter blend *tr*, then ask him to trace them and give their names, then their sounds blended together. Ask him to sound them with the long and short sounds of the vowels.

Use these words: *trail, train, trait, treat, trice, track, tram, tramp, trend, trek, trick, trill, trump, trust, tryst, try.*

If the child hesitates to pronounce the words ending in two consonants, assure him that the vowels are short, just as they are in the words ending in one consonant because there is not another vowel to make the consonant long.

Write the letter blend *tw* on the paper. Follow the same procedure, but use only long *a, e,* and *i* or short *a, e,* and *i* when sounding *tw* with vowels.

Use *tweet, twice, twang,* and *twin,* for example.

Here are some rhyming words for the child to read in columns, moving his eyes down, then up to the next list.

and	*end*	*bing*	*bank*	*drank*	*back*
band	*bend*	*king*	*lank*	*camp*	*hack*
hand	*fend*	*ming*	*rank*	*lamp*	*lack*
land	*lend*	*ping*	*sank*	*ramp*	*pack*
sand	*mend*	*ring*	*tank*	*samp*	*rack*
stand	*rend*	*sing*	*clank*	*tamp*	*sack*
	send	*wing*		*clamp*	*tack*
	vend	*swing*		*stamp*	*track*
	blend				

The child is likely to know the meaning of some of the words and can make up sentences. Sentences such as this are fun: *King Kong and I play ping-pong.*

Supplementary Activities   Have the child try to compose some sequence stories. You could write some yourself, until he has learned how to tell a series of things in the order of possible occurrence. He should be encouraged to draw upon his own experiences or experiences about which he has heard.

Example: *I had a red sled. My sled slid on the hill. I had a fast ride. I lost my cap.*

After the story has been written and read, ask the child to tell it in sequence. Start out by having him read, then tell the first two ideas, then the third, then the first three, and so on, until he can tell the entire story in sequence.

Chapter 24

QUEER VOWEL SOUNDS

It has been mentioned that when two vowels are together, the first one says its own name, and the second vowel does not say anything. Sometimes two vowels together make a different kind of sound.

A child may have difficulty learning all these different and queer sounds by rote. Familiarity with them will come gradually with practice and use. Often he will learn words containing these sounds by sight; he will know which sounds make the words "sound right." When he puts the "queer" sounds with known beginnings and endings, he usually recognizes their suitability. After he has learned to read, he will be conscious of what is needed to "make sense."

The vowel combinations that almost always conform to the pattern already learned are *ai, ay, ee, oe,* and sometimes *ea, ei, ey, ie, ou,* and *ow.* When any of these combinations are exceptions, as in *head, dead, said, weigh, eye, believe, ought,* etc., the words should be considered "learned words." They should be traced and learned by touch and sight. Such rules as "*i* before *e* except after *c,* or when sounded as *a,* as in *neighbor* and *weigh*" may also be taught as the need arises.

The combinations *eu* and *ew* are included in the group of "queer" vowels since they are a pair and break a rule; actually, they do not have *new* sounds, but the sound of long *u.*

Activities Point out the letters shown in the illustration. Say something like this to the child: "Look at these letters. There is a skull-and-crossbones over them, so they must be dangerous.

Watch out for them; they are all two-vowels-together, but you do not sound them as you did some others. The first one is not long and the next silent; instead, they get together and make a queer sound, a new or different sound."

Have the child trace the letters *a-u* and *a-w* and say their names. Then continue, "These two pairs of letters say the same thing. It is a new sound, something like you might make if you didn't like something: 'Aw, I don't like that!' Make the sound *aw*. That's right, now let's say it again."

Let the child practice the sound, then pronounce these words, as you write them: *haul, caw, law, raw, lawn, crawl, Paul, haw, paw, awl, yawn, claw.*

Say to him, "See, the *au* always has another sound after it. The *aw* sometimes has a sound after it, but not always. Say the words again."

Look at the letters *e-u* and *e-w;* have the child trace them and say their names. Say something like this: "These vowels together have the same sound as a long *u*. Sound them by saying the name of *u*. Now trace the letters again and make the sound."

Write these words, and have the child pronounce them: *feud, few, mew, new, pew, crew, flew, stew.*

Say, "See, the *eu* has to have another sound after it, but the *ew* doesn't. The *w* is at the end of the word. Say the words again."

Continue with *oi* and *oy* in the same way. Say something like this: "These pairs of vowels say the same thing. Their sound is really queer. Say the word *oil*. That's right; now take off the sound of *l*, and what is left? The sound of *oi*. *Oi* and *oy* both say the same thing."

Write these words for the child to pronounce: *oil, boil, foil, soil, toil, boy, joy, toy.*

Call his attention to the fact that *oi* always has a sound after it, but *oy* does not; a *y* or *w* usually means the end of a word or syllable.

Ask the child to trace the two *o*'s together, and say their names. Say something like this, "Sometimes the *o-o* is called a *double o*. *Double o* never says the name of *o*, and it never makes the short sound of *o*. Let's take the first *o-o*. It has a kind of a long sound, and usually sounds best with certain consonants. What sound does a cow make? Yes, *moo*. That's a rather long sound—*moooo*. Take off the sound of *m*, and what is left? Good, that's the *long* sound of double *o*."

Have the child practice the sound, then pronounce these words: *coo, goo, moo, too, woo.*

Continue, "*Double-o* at the *end* of words has the long sound. It has the long sound in these words, too.

food	*cool*	*boom*	*coon*	*coop*	*boot*
mood	*pool*	*loom*	*noon*	*loop*	*hoot*
	tool	*room*	*soon*		*loot*

Have the child trace the other pair of *o*'s and say their names. Say something like this: "These look the same, but have a short *double-o* sound. The word *good* has that sound. Say the word *good*. Now leave off the beginning sound and the ending sound, and what do you have left? The short sound of *double-o*. Say it several times."

Have the child say these words: *book, look, good, wood, wool, hook, took, hood, foot.*

If the child has trouble with this sound, have him sound the first three letters first, then add the ending sound.

Have the child trace the letters *o-u* and *o-w* and say their names. Tell him something like this: "These letters have a queer sound, too. If I were to pinch you, what might you say?" Pretend to pinch the child's arm and say, "Ow!" Continue, "That's the sound the letters make—*ow!* Now you make that sound."

Write these words: *out, bout, lout, pout, bow, cow, how, now, vow.*

As the child pronounces the words, point out that again the *w* comes at the end of words, and the *ou* has another sound after it. Tell him that there are other words containing these pairs of letters that follow the other rule he learned—when two vowels are together, the first is long, the next is silent. He can usually tell how to say them, because they wouldn't sound right with an *ow* sound.

Write these words: *low, row, flow, glow.*

After he has sounded these words with the long *o* sound, ask him if it would sound right to say, "I will stoop low to sow a row of seeds," using the *ow* sound.

Familiarity with the meaning and use of words will come very soon.

Continue with something like this: "Now look at the complete words under the skull-and-crossbones. These are words that are queer, because they don't sound the way they look. The first word sounds as if it were spelled *w-u-n*. It is the name of the first number you say when you count. Say the word. Now trace the letters, say their names, then say the word." Have the child do this several times.

Continue, "Trace the letters of the next word, and say their names. This word has the sound of a long *double-o* in it. Sound the first letter, the *t*, then make the long *double-o* sound."

Have him do the same with the word *to*. Explain that *to, too,* and *two* all sound the same. Let him write the three words.

Supplementary Activities   Write more sentences and sequence stories, using words containing the sounds already learned. Example:

I see a big boy. His name is Tom. Tom is quite a big boy. Tom has a cat. He has a bat, too. I will go out to see Tom. He may let me use his bat. He may not go home, if I go out to see him. He may let me use his bat. I can pat his cat, if I can not use his bat.

Chapter 25

QUEER CONSONANT SOUNDS

The consonant sounds *ch, sh, shr, th, thr, wh*, which all include the letter *h*, are not sounded as are the blends already presented. A different kind of sound, always containing some semblence of the *h* sound, is used. (The *ph*, of course, has the same sound as *f*.)

All except the *wh* is used at the beginning or end of a word or syllable. The sound of the *ch, th*, and *wh* varies, according to the words in which they are used.

The *ch* is nearly always stressed, as in *cheese*. In a few words, which do not appear frequently in a beginner's vocabulary, the sounds *sh* and *k* are given.

The *th* is stressed at the beginning of many words; that is, the *h* is definitely heard at the end of the sound. In a few common words that a child uses frequently, the *h* is not heard and the *th* is not stressed, as in *than, the, them, then, there, these, they, those* and *though*. For this reason, the unstressed sound must be taught, also.

Wh is given the sound of *h* in a few common words, such as *who, whose, whom*, and *whole*.

This could be a difficult lesson for the child to learn, so do not expect him to retain it all after doing it only once.

Write on your paper the consonant combinations *ch, sh, shr, th, thr, wh, ph*.

Have the child trace the letters *c-h* and say their names. Say something like this: "What are the names of these letters? Yes, *c-h*; the sounds of these letters do not blend well, so they are given a new sound. Say *choo*, the sound we might say that a train makes—choo, choo. The last part is the long *double-o* sound. Drop that part and sound just the first part. That's right, *ch*. Trace the *c-h* and make the sound—not *chuh*, only *ch*."

Ask the child to make the sound before the long, then the short vowels—*cha, che, chi, cho, chu*—then say these words: *chat, chin, chick, chuck, chain, cheek*.

Tell him that *ck* has the same sound as *k*, since *c*, before anything except *e, i*, and *y*, has the sound of *k*.

Have him trace the letters *s-h*. Say something like this: "This sound is not a blend, either. What do you say when you want someone to be quiet? You say *sh*. That's the sound of these letters when they come together. *Sh*. Make the sound. Now put the sound before the long vowel sounds—*sha, she, shi, sho, shu, shy*. Now before the short vowel sounds." Have him put the short vowel sounds before the *sh* sound—*ash, esh, ish, osh, ush*—then pronounce these words: *shad, sham, shame, shed, shell, shill, shim, shine, shod, shot, shone, shun, shut, cash, hash, lash, mash, hush, rush*.

Explain that two *l*'s sound the same as one *l*.

Teach the child the sound of *shr*, telling him that the sound of *sh* blends with the sound of *r*; he should not say *shu-r*, but *shr*. Write these words for him to pronounce: *shrive, shrove, shrill, shrub, shrug*.

Go on to the letters *th*. Say something like this: "These letters have a different sound, too; put your tongue on the edge of your upper teeth, then bring it down and back while you let the sound come out. Say the word *thanks*. Now, leave off the last part, and you will make the sound of *th*. Put that sound before the long sounds, the names of the vowels—*tha, the, thi, thu* (omit the *o*)— then before the short sound of all of the vowels."

Practice with these words: *thane, theme, thank, thick, thing, thug, with.*

Proceed in the same way with the blend *thr*, then use these words: *three, throne, thrash, thrill, throat, thrush.*

Call attention to the word under the skull-and-crossbones. Say something like this: "This is a word that you will see often when you read. You say it often when you talk. It is different because the vowel is silent, and the *th* doesn't sound quite as you have learned it. Fix your mouth the same way, but let the sound come out gently. See if you can do that." Demonstrate how this is done, so that he says *th*, not *thee*. Have him put the word *the* before the names of objects—*the pencil, the paper, the desk*. Have him trace the word and spell it, then say its name.

Practice with these words, using the unstressed sound of *th*: *the, them, then, these, those, thy.*

Ask the child to trace the letters *w-h* and say their names. Say something like this: "These letters are sounded in two ways, also. This is one way. When you ask a question, often you say, 'Why?' Say the word *why*. Now take off the long *y* sound, and you have one sound of *wh*. Try it. Trace the letters again, and make the sound." Have him combine this stressed sound with the long and short vowel sound in *what, whe, whi, who.*

Use these words for practice: *whale, wheel, whoa, whine, white, wham, when, while, whip.*

Have the child trace the letters *w-h* again and say to him, "Sometimes these letters have the same sound as *h* has. In this word, give the letters *wh* the sound of *h*: *whole*." Write the word, so he can trace it and say it.

"Look at the other word under the skull-and-crossbones. The *wh* has the sound of *h*, and the *o* has the sound of the long *double o*. That's the sound in *moo*. Trace the word, say the letters, then sound it: say *hoo*.

"Now I'll write the words *whom* and *whose*. They are words to watch, too; they start out the same way with the sound of *h*, then the long *double-o* sound, then the consonant sound. You say the words *whom* and *whose*. Remember, the *s* has the sound of *z;* there is no sound after it."

Have the child look at the letters *p-h*, trace them and say their names. Tell him something like this, "These letters are not blends, either; they have the sound of *f*. When you see these letters together, just pretend they are *f*. The sound is the same."

Let the child pronounce these words: *phone, graph.*

Supplementary Activities Continue to compose sentence. For a change, questions and answers could be written.

Examples: *Who is that? It is I. Did you go home? Yes, I went home. What did you see? I saw my cat.*

If words having some similarity are configured, as demonstrated earlier, the child will be more likely to recall their beginning sounds. Draw lines around these words:

what   that   who   how   when   then

Chapter 26

SILENT CONSONANTS

Silent letters appear in many words, sometimes apparently without purpose. The silent *e* at the end of most words is usually placed there to show that another vowel is long. The second of two vowels together often denotes the same thing. The consonants *gh* may do this, also.

In some words, such as *ghost*, the *h* is silent; in *hymn*, the *n* is not sounded.

The combinations *kn, gn, pn, rh,* and *wr* present blending difficulty, so the first letters are not sounded. Most words containing these are leftovers from Old English, usually through Greek or the Teutonic languages. For the common words that a child encounters, it is enough to know that, since the sounds can not be put together smoothly, he ignores the first letter and sounds the second one. He will soon become familiar with them.

The letter *l* is silent in a few common words; usually its presence in the word affects the sound of the *a* that precedes it, as in *calm* and *palm.*

Any less common silent letters can be handled as they appear. Write on your paper the word-combinations: *kn, gn, wr.* Also write *lf, lm, gh.*

Have the child look at the first group of letters. Say something like this: "These letters are consonants put together, but they are not blends. They don't make a new sound, either; you sound the second one only. What will you sound in the first pair? Yes, the *n;* in the second, the *n;* and in the next, the *r.* Let's write the letters again on the paper, then you cross out the first letters. Make a line through the *k*, *g*, and *w*. That's right. Now trace the letters and give their sounds: *kn-n, gn-n, wr-r*. Good." Then you can have the student write these words for practice:

knee	*knave*	*knack*	*knit*	*knock*	*know*
kneel	*knife*	*knelt*	*knob*		*known*
gnat	*gnash*	*gnome*	*gnu*		
wren	*write*	*wrote*	*wrath*	*wring*	*wrung*

Now have the child look at the letters *l-f* and *l-m*. Say something like this: "When these letters are together and there is an *a* before them, the *l* is silent. Make just the sound of *f* and *m*."

Write these words, and have him cross out the *l*'s, then say the words: *calf, half*.

Now write these words, and have him cross out the *l*'s: *calm, palm*.

Then say, "In these words, the *l* makes the *a* say *ah*. When the doctor wants to look at your throat, he tells you to open your mouth and say, 'ah.' You make that sound when you say these words. Say the words again."

The child will come across this sound in other words later. Call attention to the next letter combination, the *gh*. Say something like this: "Sometimes, these letters act the way a vowel does. They make the vowel before it say its own name." Write these words on the paper: *bright, fight, knight, light, might, night, plight, right, sight, tight*.

Have the child draw lines through the *g* and *h* to show that they are silent, then pronounce the words. The older children could trace the letters of each word, and learn to spell it.

Supplementary Activities   Write more sentences and configure difficult words.

Examples: *I know who that is. It is Pam. Pam and I like to play. We play with a calf. The calf is not half as big as we are, but it can run fast. It makes us laugh.*

Tell the child that the *gh* in *laugh* has the sound of *f* and the *au* is almost like a short *a*. Say something like this, "This word, *laugh*, is a skull-and-crossbones word. Write it on the paper, and draw a line around the shape of the letters. I'll show you how to configure or draw it, then you do it. Trace the letters, say their names, then say the word. See if you can learn how to spell *laugh*."

Write some sentences with *gh* words.

Example: *It is not right to fight with the knight,* or *I might see a bright light at night.*

Chapter 27

THE VOWELS WITH L AND R

Most of the unusual sounds of letters seem to be involved with the letters *l* and *r*. The sounds of these letters themselves do not change, but they affect those of the vowel that they follow. The *r* placed after each vowel actually makes a blend.

A before *r* produces a sound that is the same as the name of the letter *r*. When used within a word, it usually has that same sound. When used as a suffix, a syllable at the end of a word, it has the same sound as *er, ir,* and *ur;* at the beginning of some words, it has the sound of *air.*

In one-syllable words, *er, ir,* and *ur* all have the same sound. At the beginning of some words, *er* has the sound of *air,* and *ir* has the sound of *ear.* The sound of *ur* is pretty consistently the same, except when it is in a word with a "magic *e.*" *O* before *r* has almost a long sound, even when it is in a word without the "magic *e.*" In unaccented syllables, *or* usually has the same sound as *ur,* as do *ar, er,* and *ir.*

Write down on the paper the combinations *ar, er, ir, or* and *ur.*

Have the child put his finger on the *a-r* and say the names of the letters. Say something like this, "The sound of these letters is the same as the name of the letter *r.* Make the sound. Now put the sound after some consonant sounds."

Write these letters, and have the child make the sounds: *bar, car, dar, far, gar, har, jar, kar, lar, mar, nar, par, sar, tar, var, yar, zar.*

Then write these words, and let him pronounce them: *bar, car, far, jar, mar, tar, bard, card, hard, lard, bark, lark, park, barn, darn.*

Since any word that contains the name of *r* always has the letters *ar* in it, it is safe to allow the child to think of more words like this.

Have the child look at the letters *er*, *ir*, and *ur*. Say something like this: "These letter combinations usually sound alike. Sometimes when a person is cold, he might say, 'B-r-r-r, it's cold!' Now make that sound; then, take off the *b* sound and what have you left? Yes, that's the sound that these letter-combinations make. Make the sound again. Put the sound of some consonants before the sound. Say *ber, der, fer, her, ker, ler, mer, ner, per, ser, ter, ver, wer, yer, zer.* That's right. The sounds are the same, whether the letters are *er*, *ir*, or *ur*."

Write these words for the child to sound: *her, herd, fir, sir, stir, bird, burr, cur, fur, purr, curd, curl.*

Let the child trace the letters *o-r* and tell their names. Say something like this: "Sometimes you might say, 'Give me this or that. I want an apple or an orange.' When you say the word *or*, you are making the sound of the letters *o-r*. Sound the letters. Put the sounds of some consonants before *or*; start with *b* again, and go through the alphabet: *bor, cor, dor, for, gor, hor, jor, kor, lor, mor, nor, por, sor, tor, vor, wor, zor.*"

Write these words and have the child pronounce them: *bore, core, for, fore, lore, more, pore, sore, wore, cord, ford, born, corn, morn, fort, port.*

Explain that the "magic *e*" does *not* change the sound.

Continue, "Now, look at the skull-and-crossbones words. There's something different about those words. The *ar* in the first word has the sound of the letter *r* even though there is an *e* on the end. Say the word. It is one you use often, as when you say, 'How are you?' The next word has an *ar* in it, but the sound is like that of *or*. Say the word. The next word has an *ou* in it, but is pronounced like *for*. The word *four* is the one you say when you count one, two, three, *four*. Trace the letters in the word *four*, say their names, then say the word."

If you want the child to learn to spell the word, have him trace it and say the letters and then the name of the word several times.

You could have him learn the words *word* and *world*, which contain the *ur* sound, also.

Supplementary Activities   Configure the words:

there	*here*	*where*
their	*hear*	*were*

Have the child learn the words by tracing and pronouncing them.

Be sure that the child pays particular attention to the beginning of the words *where* and *there, where* and *were*. Stress the various sounds of *ere*.

The older children may benefit from these explanations: "*There* and *their* both start out with *the*. Remember that, when you are writing them. *There* means *in that place. Their* tells you that something belongs to *them*. If you are an *heir*, something will some day belong to you. The word *their* contains the word *heir*. *Here* means *in this place. Hear* tells you what your *ear* does. The word *ear* can be found in *hear*."

Write, or have the child write more sentences. Examples: *Where are you? Where were you? You were here. You were there. Birds fly here and there.*

The letter *l* also changes the sounds of vowels in some words. Before *double-l*, the sounds of *a* and *u* are sometimes changed; before *ld* and *lk*, the *i* and *o* are often long rather than short, as might be expected. The vowel *e* is not affected by the *l* or by the *n*.

Write on your paper the following two groups of letter combinations: *all, alt, ull; ild, old, olk.*

Say something like this: "Look at these letter groups. Say the names of the letters in each. Which letter is in each group? Yes, the *l*. Why do you suppose we should put the skull-and-crossbones above those letters? Of course. There's something different about the sounds. Usually the vowel before two consonants is short. Before these consonants, the vowel has another sound. The *a* has the sound of *aw*. Sound the word *all*. That's right, like *awl* and *awlt*. The *u* before two *l*'s is like the short *double-o* sound; say it, like the *oo* in *good*, it is *oo-l*."

Write these words, and have the child pronounce them: *all, ball, call, fall, gall, hall, tall, wall, halt, malt, salt, bull, full, pull.*

In many words, the *u* has a short sound before *double-l*. Have the child pronounce these words: *cull, dull, gull, hull, lull, mull.*

Continue, "Look at the other group of letters. What letter is in each of those? Yes, the *l* again. You would expect the vowels to be short, wouldn't you, since they are followed by two consonants? They are not; they say their own name in most words when they are followed by the consonants *ld* or *lk*."

Write these words for the child to pronounce: *mild, wild, child, bold, cold, gold, hold, mold, sold, told, folk, yolk.*

Write these words, and explain that other consonants sometimes make the *i* and *o* long: *bind, find, kind, mind, grind, pint, host, most, post, both.*

Other words can be found in additional lists in the appendix.

Supplementary Activities   Have the child try to compose some nonsense rhymes.

Examples:
> *The child is tall*
> *But he may fall*
> *If he throws the ball*
> *At the wall.*

> *He was old*
> *And bold*
> *When he sold*
> *The gold.*

Have the child try to read some nursery rhymes or simple stories from books. If there are words that he cannot "sound out" for himself, tell him what they are so the line of thought will not be interrupted.

Help him to memorize some of the rhymes and short poems. Have him repeat the first line, then the second, then the first and second, and so on.

Chapter 28

UNEXPECTED SHORT
VOWEL SOUNDS

This group of vowels is among the most difficult, because there is no precedent for them that can be explained to a child. However, most of them do fall into a pattern; they appear so frequently in similar words that the unexpected becomes expected now and then. The words containing them should be treated as "learned words." Meeting some of these irregularities now will prepare the child for the possibility of unusual situations that may occur in any situation throughout his life.

Giving the *e* before an *a* a short sound instead of a long sound gradually becomes natural in some words; giving *o* the sound of short *u* will come easily when it is found in so many ordinary words, such as *of, from,* and *love.*

Say, "Look at the letters under the skull-and-crossbones. What are the first letters? Yes, *ea.* In some words, *ea* has the sound of short *e.* Here are some of those words."

Write the words: *head, dead, meant, health, wealth.*

Have the child pronounce the words, then say something like this: "There are some words that look the same and can be pro-

nounced two different ways. Sometimes the *e* is short, and sometimes the *e* is long, depending on how you use the word."

Write these words, and have the child pronounce them both
ways. Explain the difference in meaning:

   read, read   lead, lead

Write these words:

   read, red   lead, led

Continue, "Words spelled differently may sound the same, too.
Say the words." Explain the meanings of these words, also.

Have the child look at the word *said* under the skull-and-crossbones. Ask him to trace the letters and say their names. Say something like this: "This is a word to watch. The *ai* has the sound of
short *e*, too. Say the word. That's right. It's so different that you
should be sure to remember what it is!"

Say something like this: "Why do you suppose the letter *o* would
be put under a skull-and-crossbones? It's because in so many words
it sounds like another letter. It has the sound of short *u* in many
words."

Write these words: *of, come, some, from, son, ton, month, love,
dove, shove.*

Other words with this sound of *o* can be found in the appendix.
They should be traced, and learned by touch and sight.

Supplementary Activities   Call attention to these facts about
the letters discussed in the preceding lesson:

1. The *ea* sounded as short *e* is often followed by *d* and *lth*.
Ear often has the sound of *er*, as in *heard* and *earl*.

2. The *o* having a short *u* sound is often followed by *ve* and *th*.

Write sentences to illustrate the sounds learned.

I read a book.

He heard me.

I hurt my head.

It is good to have both health and wealth. (Call attention to the
short *a* in have.)

*I love my pets. I have a glove on my hand. My hat is on the top
of my head.*

Do not take my pets from me.

I read a red book. I read well. I know I can read well. I broke my lead. I can lead the line well. I led the line. (Many words can be recognized by association, and by anticipating the most obvious meaning. The wrong pronunciation of the words would not make sense.)

Form these words, calling attention to the beginning and ending sounds: *of, from, for.*

Chapter **29**

TRICK BRICKS AND SYLLABLES

The words given so far have been one-syllable words. Words of more than one syllable do not present difficult problems once one knows these basic facts:

1. Accented syllables usually conform to the same patterns as words of one syllable.

2. If an accented syllable ends in a vowel, that vowel is long.

3. If an accented syllable ends in a consonant, the preceding vowel is short.

4. The vowels in unaccented syllables are given an indefinite sound similar to that of short *u*. Some dictionaries indicate the sound with a *schwa* (ə); others show a short *u*.

The spelling of unaccented syllables becomes a matter of visual and tactual memory of vowels.

Common prefixes and suffixes soon are part of a child's store of knowledge, which is retained and can be recalled when needed without conscious effort.

Write these words: *tag, hem, sip, sob.*

Say something like this: "Do these words have long or short vowels? Yes, they are short. If you were to put an *e* at the end, what would happen to the vowels? The vowel would be long. What is the first word? *Tag.* If you wanted to say you tagged some-one, you would have to put the letters *ed* on the word, but if you did that the vowel would be long. Look at the first word in the illustration. Spell it. It has two *g*'s. We call the second *g* a 'trick brick,' because it is put there to keep the *e* from hopping over to

166

make the *u* long. Now say the word and add the sound of *d* to *tag*. That's right, *tagged*. Now, do the same with the other words."

Let the child write the words *hemmed, sipped,* and *sobbed,* then say them.

Write these words, have the child put in the "trick bricks," and add *ed: bat, pet, fit.*

Say something like this: "Some consonants are hard to sound together; *t* and *d* are like that, so you must use your voice twice. Say *bat-ted, pet-ted, fit-ted.* Watch for sounds like that when you say words that end in *ed.*

Those words have two syllables, like two beats of your heart—first one, then the next. Say the word again; the last part sounds like a short *u* before the *d.*"

Write these words: *bat, beg, sit, dot, run.*

Continue, "Are the vowels in these words long or short? Yes, they are short. Say the words. Suppose you wanted to say 'I am batting a ball.' You would have to put the letters *ing* on the word *bat.* An *i* would make that *a* long, too, so you need a 'trick brick.' Write the word *batting,* just as it is in the illustration."

Have the child write and pronounce the words *batting, begging, sitting, dotting,* and *running.*

Write the words: *lame, name, smile.*

Say something like this: "What kind of sounds have the vowels in these words? Yes, they are long. They don't need any 'trick bricks,' but you can't put two vowels together either; that would make the silent *e* long. Just take it off, it doesn't have to be there at all, since it doesn't say anything." Have the child write and pronounce the words *lamed, named, smiled, laming, naming, smiling.*

Continue, "Look at the last word in the illustration. You can't say that with one beat of your voice. You sound the first part, as far as the first *p*, then the last part. The two *p*'s make that first vowel short. Every syllable must have a vowel, just as every one-syllable word must have a vowel. What is the vowel in that last part? Yes, the *y*. A *y* on the end of a word of more than one syllable has the sound of short *i*. When you say it on the end, it sounds almost like a long *e*. Now say the word, *hap-py*. Good."

Write these words, and let the child pronounce them: *pret-ty, hur-ry, par-ty, for-ty*.

Supplementary Activities   Now that syllables have been introduced, there are not many words that the child cannot "sound out." The proper accent is of great importance, but many of the words in beginning reading are familiar to a child's ears and are likely to be correctly accented. The child will eventually learn these facts:

1. Stress is usually placed on the root or most important part of a word.

2. In verbs of two syllables, the accent is usually placed on the last syllable; in other two-syllable words, it is usually on the first. Example: *pre-sent'; pres'ent*.

3. In longer words, the accent is most often placed on the antepenult—that is, the last but two of the syllables. Example: *pre-sent'a ble*.

Familiarity with the right sound of the English language takes care of many pronunciation problems.

Nonsense sentences like these may help the child to establish the rules for adding suffixes:

I found a thin dime in the diner when I ate dinner.

I hoped I could see you hopping, but you were stopping and stooping.

If the child does not know the word *could*, let him trace it and learn it visually.

Other sentences containing words of more than one syllable may be composed.

Examples:

He is very happy. Hear him singing.

We are playing ball.

Did you ever play ball?

I never saw you playing.

Even I can play ball.
I will present you with a present on your birthday.

Configure these words, and call attention to their beginning sounds: *ever, never, very, even.*

Check the words for similarities and differences.

Chapter 30

SUMMING UP

As you and your child read together, you will find that the sentences that are the easiest for him to understand are those that conform to the correct patterns of grammar and those with the proper punctuation.

Beginning readers are usually not much concerned with formal grammatical terms or with the names of punctuation symbols. Whether or not your child has started to learn grammar in his particular school system at the age level covered in the preceding lessons, it would be wise to mention occasionally such words as "noun," "verb," "period," and "comma" as the child reads. By so doing, you will be building a background that will be very helpful in his later studies. It may also stimulate his reading from a practical standpoint. But on no account should technical terms be allowed to interfere with the child's pure enjoyment of reading for its own sake.

Even though your child may have learned letters, sounds, sentence structure, configurations, and story reconstruction, he may still not be a good reader. If this is so, perhaps the reason lies in the fact that he has not learned to *enjoy* reading. There are remedies for that, too, which the following suggestions may help.

1. The easy poetry, nursery rhymes, and riddles mentioned earlier are often valuable. The lines are short, so his eyes are more easily controlled; he can "swing" through them and learn to match his personal rhythm to the beat and cadence of the words.

2. Go through the reading material with the child. Pick out words or "spots" that he finds difficult, and help him with them.

He can then read it to himself several times and later perform for you and others, catching the rhythm from the repetition. Young children love to read over and over again something they like and can read well.

3. Older children are not given sufficient opportunity for practicing repetition. A tape recorder is one answer to that lack. The older student can read into it, play it back, and find his mistakes as he follows the same material in his book. He can discover where his reading needs rephrasing and smoothing before he makes a final recording. A tape recorder will do much for a younger child, too. A parent can tape poetry, stories, or other selections and use them as a library from which the child can choose the things he likes best. Some children enjoy hearing a selection that has fairly apparent word changes or substitutions; they like to find the place in the book where the tape has made a "mistake."

4. If the child persists in making a mistake with a certain word, note the word and write it on a rough paper towel for him to trace before he starts to read.

5. Give the child an opportunity to move his eyes across the page from left to right, back to the left and down, and across the page again, in the reading movement, for a few minutes before he starts to read for you. It will also help if you move your finger back and forth on the page he is going to read and have him follow it with his eyes.

6. Have the child read a little just before going to sleep at night and again the first thing in the morning. Reading a short poem or riddle just before and after sleep makes the following day's lessons easier by insuring the cooperation of his senses.

When a child can decode the abstractions of words and phrases easily and smoothly, the joy of reading is boundless. Your problem then will be to pry him away from a book! No matter what grade your child is in, he will be able to cope with any situation that requires an ability to read well.

PART IV

LEARNING THE CONCEPT AND USE OF NUMBERS

INTRODUCTION

Mathematics is the study of the properties dealing with measurements and the relation of quantities. It is a science (the word itself comes from the Greek *mathematikos,* referring to science), and as such, it has its own exact vocabulary.

Arithmetic, the most elementary part of mathematics, is an introduction to the field, in which the student learns about the tools for reckoning, for counting, and for calculating, and the correct way to use them.

Before the tools themselves are put to use, it is necessary that the *concept* of numbers be completely understood. Number is the sum total of things in a group or series. It is an entity that has a real existence of its own—an essential nature apart from that to which it is applied. For instance, *two* does not have to be two persons or two tables; it can be a concept by itself.

To speak of *one* object is another way of saying *an* object. In fact, the word *one* comes from the old English word *an.* Beyond one, the names of the numbers describe *sets* of things. There are, of course, sets of two, three, four and so on, up to the infinite numbers, those so large they cannot be counted.

Numerals are the names or symbols used to represent these sets, devices enabling us to count. Although Roman numerals are still employed occasionally, we generally use words and Arabic figures to describe the numbers.

Apart from knowing the values, names, meanings, and symbols of the numbers as entities, a student must be conversant with the *abstract* concepts of them. Before he can achieve basic skills with numerals, he must have advanced beyond the laborious, fumbling steps of counting.

For instance, he must be able to recognize *four* in any of its groupings—2 and 2, 3 and 1, 1 and 3, 0 and 4, 4 and 0.

He must be able to understand these concepts as they apply to all manner of objects as well as abstractions. He must know the *names* for these amounts, the symbols for them, and their various forms.

He must be able to understand the cardinal numbers—one, two, three, etc.—and the ordinals—those used in stating the order of things, such as first, second, third, and fourth. Then there are the "teens" for the digit numbers plus ten; the "ty's" for the digit numbers times ten; the "th's" for the fractional parts and the ordinals.

The concept of six, for example, will clarify the concepts of sixteen, sixty, and sixth.

Once the child has learned these basic fundamentals, he will be able to understand the reasons as well as the processes involved in addition, multiplication, subtraction, and division. The number combinations will appear logical and sequential.

Occasionally, there are spots along the road to mathematics that seem to be insurmountable roadblocks. For some reason, these vary with different children. For one child, the problem may be addition or multiplication. For another, it will be subtraction or division. Others may bog down completely on factors and multiples, long division, fractions, decimals, or even the vocabulary.

A number of activities can be undertaken in the home for the purpose not only of learning the basic skills, but of breaking down any mental barriers that may exist.

In this section of the learning program you will find, among others, sections devoted to some of the more difficult problems your child will face in school—specifically, analyzing numbers, filling in missing numbers in a sequence, and the logical methods for solving "story problems."

At the outset, the vocabulary of mathematics may seem to be an entirely new language. But words, many of them hundreds of years old and derived from many ancient tongues, are used with reason. When a child becomes familiar with these reasons, he is more likely to remember them. This, added to his previously acquired skills of reading with understanding and thinking logically and sequentially, will put him a long way along the road to complete understanding of mathematics as both a science and a vital tool in his everyday life.

Chapter 31

COUNTING

It is most important that you look for activities that will give your child of preschool age experiences with the basic number concepts; be sure that he understands the sequence of numbers as they grow larger and smaller.

One way to do this is to use steps. If you have no steps available, take a piece of oilcloth about eleven feet long and mark it off into eleven parts, numbering the sections 0 through 10.

Have the child stand on the zero, then count each step as he proceeds to ten; then count backward, as he returns to zero.

A set of sturdy steps with one-inch risers, made in the form of a stile, would be ideal for a child's outdoor play, especially if you put the numbers going up on one side and those going down on the other. The even numbers could be put on the right side of each step, the odd numbers on the left.

Many activities can be performed on the steps or on the indoor oilcloth strip. For example, you can ask the child which number will come after the particular step he is on, and which came before. This prepares him for his first-grade work with number abstractions and, incidentally, with their symbols.

If you instruct him to go up five steps and tell you how many more steps he must go before he reaches ten, he is already learning to add and subtract. You can vary the instructions in as many ways as there are addition and subtraction combinations of the numbers one through ten.

You might put the words "Count Down" on the top step near

the side where he will be counting down from ten to one; this will give him an idea of the meaning of the term "count-down."

The same activities could be performed on the oilcloth strip.

If your child is a little older, you could let him learn the concept of "minus" numbers. Make another strip, number it from −1 through −10; turn it around so that the −1 is next to the zero and the numbers proceed in a direction opposite to that of the first strip.

Tell the child that there are numbers below zero. He can "count-down" here, too, but the numbers will be larger as they go farther and farther down. If he steps forward from zero and proceeds two steps on the plus numbers, then goes back four steps, he will be on the −2.

Thus he is adding or combining + and − numbers. $2 - 4 = -2$.

Ask him to examine the strips and see the differences between +4 and −2. It is 6 steps. The difference between numbers is subtraction. 4 minus a $-2 = 6$.

This will help your child to understand problems in *temperatures below zero*.

Much later he will be able to understand some of the concepts of algebraic expressions. He will be proud that he understands them and perhaps wonder why others do not. You will then count as a good investment the time you spend with him now.

After your child thoroughly understands, and can manipulate, the number concepts to ten, it is expedient to give him more experience with odd and even numbers.

Again, he needs concrete objects at the outset. In this case, they should be solid objects, ones not made of removable parts. Silverware, kitchen utensils, books, and pieces of clothing are all sensible tools for this kind of learning.

MATERIALS NEEDED

1. Five pairs each of socks, shoes, mittens, gloves, books.
2. Or models of them cut from paper.

Activities   Say something like this: "Let's see which of these sets of things we can share equally; we'll start with this sock. Can you have this sock if I have it? No, either you have it or I have it;

we cannot share it unless we cut it into pieces; then it wouldn't be good for either of us. Here is its mate. You take that and I'll keep this; you have one and I have one. Is that an even number, shared between us? Yes, there were two, so we each could have one. When there are two things, so that two people can share them equally, the number is even. One is not even, because we could not share the one, but two is even.

"Now let's put that pair of socks together again and put another sock with it. How many socks are there here now? Yes, three. Can we share these socks equally? No, we'd have one left over, an 'odd' sock. There would be a pair and an odd one. Is three an even or an odd number? That's right, it is odd."

Continue with this routine until the child has seen all the odds and evens through ten. Use different objects to insure his full comprehension. Call his attention to the pattern of odds and evens; first odd, then even, next odd, then even; or first even, then odd.

The evens will give him the answers to the multiplication tables of twos to 2×5. He could also learn that two twos are four, three twos are six, four twos are eight, and so on.

Chapter 32

NUMBERS AND SETS 1–10

We are fortunate in having a number system based on ten. There are only ten values that must be learned as concepts, only ten figures that must be made to represent those concepts.

The zero has no value as a counting number and must be perceived as representing no number at all, but also as a component part of ten and the multiples of ten.

If your child does not yet have a clear understanding of numbers and sets as entities, have him perform the following activity.

MATERIALS NEEDED

1. Paper and pencils.
2. At least ten of any type of object, such as blocks or spoons.
3. Any other toys or objects available.

Activities Draw a circle, a square, and a line on a piece of paper.

Say something like this: "What do you see on the paper? Yes, a circle, a square, a line. When you say *a* that means the same as *one*. There is one circle, one square, one line. Give me one block. That's right. Now, give me one ball, one doll (name any objects available). How many pencils do I have in my hand? That's right, one."

Make another circle, another square, another line on the paper and continue: "Now, I've made one more of each of these figures. That makes a set of circles, a set of squares, a set of lines. There are two in each set. Can you give me a set of blocks that will match these sets? A set of balls? A set of dolls? That's good. See if you can find any other sets like these. How about your hands? Is that a set of two? Yes, and your feet."

Let him go on to point out two eyes, two ears, two chairs, and so on, using the word *two* each time.

Continue with sets of three by adding one more of each of your drawings. Tell him the name of that set. Go on through all of the numbers to ten.

Try to find some sets of each that are common and obvious. The sets of four will be easy; he can point out the legs of chairs, tables, etc., and can recall many four-legged animals. The fives are easy, too, because of the fingers and toes, and the tens as well. The others—three, six, eight, and nine—can be represented by fingers or groups of objects. This is a good time to show that two twos are four, two threes are six, two fives are ten, three sets of three are nine, three sets of two are six, five sets of two are ten, and so on.

Do not make the symbols representing the amounts at this time. Have him absorb the concept of number in each set or combination of sets.

Have him take one object, such as a block, and place another one beside it as he says "two." Continue in sequence until he reaches ten, then have him take them away one at a time and say the names.

Have him divide the objects into groups of two and five, then take nine, and divide that set into sets of three.

Nothing need be said about the processes used—just let him see how the combinations work out. He need not be asked to memorize any of the things he has learned in this lesson. Try it again later and find out how much he has retained.

Give the child opportunities to tell you which of certain groups has the largest quantity of objects, which is the larger in amount, which is the lesser or smaller. It will save your child untold hours of learning the "combinations" by rote if you reinforce here the different groupings that result in "constant" numbers. For instance, no matter what the order or sequence, $4 + 1$, $1 + 4$, $2 + 3$, and $3 + 2$ will always result in the same constant value of five.

The idea that five objects can be placed in one tight group made up of the various combinations is often puzzling to some children. A balance scales is of great value to show this. If you put five spoons on either side of the scales you can place them in different patterns on one side and in a constant group of five on the other. The child needs to try this out for himself, on and off the scales, to be sure.

Crayons and paper or a series of cards can also be of great value in showing the child that position in groups makes no change in the amount. Three objects drawn in a straight line from left to right, with two added farther to the right, are five, as well as two objects at the top of a space with three below them. Later the child will understand instantly that the placement of numbers in addition problems can differ, as in:

$$3 + 2 = 5, \qquad 2 + 3 = 5, \qquad \begin{array}{r} 2 \\ +3 \\ \hline 5 \end{array} \qquad \begin{array}{r} 3 \\ +2 \\ \hline 5 \end{array} \qquad \text{etc.}$$

He will need to know later that the symbols representing five also may differ (5, five, V) with the value unaffected.

Be sure he knows that all the numbers he is learning are *counting* numbers. They are *whole* numbers also, but he need not be concerned with this unless he is dealing with fractions.

When your child is ready to learn to make the *digits*—at about the same time he is learning the names of the *letters* and how to make them—have similar squared paper ready for this task. *Digit,* from the Latin word *digitus* meaning *finger* or *toe,* is the name given the Arabic figures used to represent numbers. The name is appropriate, for the decimal system of numbers is based on the number of fingers given to man.

Paper can be lined or it can be folded into squares of the right size for making the digits.

The strokes follow the same general pattern of lines drawn downward and those that curve to the right or left. The curves for the zero and nine go toward the left; for the eight, both ways; for the two, three, and five, to the right.

HOW TO MAKE THE DIGITS

The exact size and shape of the digits varies in different systems. Very young children are allowed to make them large and round. As cursive writing is adopted, the size and slant of the digits is expected to change also. Any extra curves can be added when they are needed.

Many children can remember on which side the shapes are open, if you tell them that two, three, five, and seven have their mouths open and could bite the ones before them. If any number gives a child difficulty, make it on a paper towel and have him trace its shape as he says its name.

Children rarely tire of making the digits, especially if you emphasize sequence and allow them to draw the appropriate number of objects beside them.

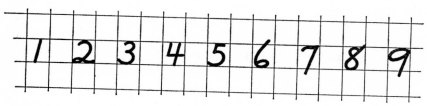

Have the child look at the shapes and notice the likes and differences. Say something like this: "The six begins a little above the top middle line; the seven and nine ends a little below the bottom middle line. The zero is the only one that is a circle; the nine has an oval-shaped top, and six has a smaller oval at the bottom; the one, four, five, seven, and nine have straight lines; if you look, you can see something like an s in the eight; you will have to pick up your pencil once while making the four, and the five, too, to make it correctly."

You can continue: "Make a circle for the zero. The one begins near the center of the middle square and slants a little towards the left—just a straight slanted line down to the bottom of the square.

"The two also starts near the center, curves around toward the right, a little curve, around to the left, all the way over to the side of the square, now makes a loop and curves around back to the right. The three starts near the center, curves around to the right, then to the left, makes a little point, and curves around again. Make a bigger curve and go all the way around to the left.

"The four starts at the left of the square, slants down, not all the way—go straight across to the right of the square. Now lift your pencil and put it at the top right of the square and make a line down just as you make a one.

"Now the five. Start at the top center of the square, go straight down, just a little way, curve around to the right and go all the way to the left. Lift your pencil and put it at the top of that straight line. Make a line across to the right. That's the correct way to make a five.

"Start the six a little above the middle square. Don't make a straight line down—curve it a little toward the left, then around to the right; at the bottom of the square, make a little loop, go back to the left.

"Start the seven at the top of the square, near the left, go toward the right, make a little point, and slant down, as if you were making a one; go a little below the bottom middle line.

"To make the eight, start at the right, curve around to the left and go back to the right in the middle of the square. That's something like a printed letter s. Now curve upward, then slant to the right. (Some make the eight around the other way. Whichever way is easier for the child is satisfactory, provided he makes it with one continuous line.)

"The nine starts near the top right of the square. Make an oval, then start as if you were making a circle, but make it thinner; go around to the left, then to the right, close it up; then make a straight slanted line down, just as you did for a seven, a little below the bottom of the square. To make a ten, make a one, then a zero, close together."

Chapter 33

SIGNS

The meaning of the signs used with the four processes is one of the first things that a child should learn. Make them on paper.

After making them on your work paper, say something like this: "When numbers are to be made larger, a sign with two lines is used. The lines cross to show that the numbers are put together. This addition sign is called *plus*. One line is horizontal (it follows the horizon) the other is vertical (it points toward the top, the vertex). One line is added to another.

"The multiplication or times sign has the two lines, but they are slanted. They look like the sign for a railroad crossing, where the trains go by many times.

"The sign that means to subtract is the simplest of them all. One straight horizontal line means to take one number away from one other number, to make the first number smaller in value.

"The other sign tells us to make a number smaller by division, to separate it into parts. It has only one line also, with a dot above and below. It tells us to put one number into another, over and over again. We could keep subtracting it, but that would take us a long time.

"The other sign is a very important one: the 'equals' sign. Equal means *alike* or *the same*." Show the child the two parallel lines that mean *equals*. Point out that they are the same length.

Then go on: "Look at this problem. $2 + 2 = 4$. See the little mark I have put under the equals sign? That is like the *fulcrum* of a scale." If you have a balance scales, show him the fulcrum, and explain that this supports the two sides. The amount of weight on each side must be equal to make the scales balance.

"If you put more on one side of the fulcrum, you must put the same amount on the other. $2 + 2 + 2 = 6$; $4 \times 2 = 8$; $6 = 6$; $8 = 8$.

"If you take some off one side, you must take the same amount off the other side. $2 \times 2 - 2 = 2$; $4 - 2 = 2$."

If you have been using a scales, put some objects on one side, until they balance; take some off each side until they balance again.

Most children can "play" with scales for long periods of time with sustained interest, balancing stones, shells, small toys and any other available objects.

The concepts gained are invaluable for an understanding of problem solution, and later, of formulas and equations.

Chapter 34

PREHISTORIC MAN GAME TO TEACH COUNTING

Very soon after a child has learned his way around in the concepts of numbers up to ten, he is ready to hear the story of how his prehistoric ancestors might have handled "counting." Early man could have used his ten fingers for communicating amounts of one through ten, but he surely would have had occasion to deal with larger amounts.

MATERIALS NEEDED

1. Have a pile of about 30 stones or other small objects (or paper markers).

2. Draw a circle or square large enough to enclose about 30 toy goats; if these are not available, you could cut out animal shapes or use small pieces of paper to represent the goats.

3. Draw two pairs of parallel lines to represent ditches, long enough to hold a row of ten stones or other markers.

Activities Say something like this: "No one knows exactly how humans began to count. We do know that the cave man must have kept track of the number of goats he owned. He probably used his fingers until he came to ten, but when he needed higher amounts, he was in trouble. Some very clever ancestor of ours may have worked it out this way."

Have the child look at the materials you have gathered and explain to him what they represent.

Continue: "Imagine two prehistoric men who are ready to trade some animals and tools. One man has many goats, the other has

187

tools—more, perhaps, than he has fingers. A big pile of stones has been collected, and two ditches have been dug.

"We'll pretend that we are the prehistoric men. Suppose the tool-man has held up his ten fingers twice, and then four fingers of one hand to show how many goats he wants for his tools.

"This is the way the goats were counted. Now you be the goat-man. Let one goat out of the pen and put one stone in the right-hand ditch. Bend one finger over to keep track. Let out another goat, put another stone into the same ditch, bend another finger."

Have the child continue until all ten fingers have been bent over. He can use first one hand, then the other, so that one will be available for moving the goats and stones; or you could do the moving for him.

After all ten fingers have been used, take another stone and put it in the next ditch to the left. This ditch, is the *tens*-ditch; the first one is the *ones* or *units*-ditch. Clear out the ones ditch, because these ten goats are now counted in the tens-ditch.

Have the child stretch out his ten fingers, with hands flat on the table; put a stone at each of the fingertips so he'll know that there was a stone for each finger. Then continue: "One stone, one finger, two stones, two fingers, and so on. The prehistoric man knows, now, that he has let out as many goats as he has fingers."

Have the child go through this again so he has two stones in the tens-ditch; then four more in the ones-ditch, symbolized by four stones and four fingers. He has given the tool-man the number of goats he asked for. We would say two tens plus four ones, or twenty-four.

The tool-man would count his tools in the same way.

Make up more stories involving different amounts until the child understands the concept of tens. With more stones and another ditch, this could go on into the hundreds. He could find the composition of such numbers as 653—six hundreds, five tens, and three ones. Arrange sometimes to have no ones, or no tens, so that the child will understand such numbers as 50, 605, or 210.

You may have to play these games with your child many times. It is a rare child who will not want to repeat the procedure over and over again. This activity will lead easily into reading and writing large numbers.

Here is another activity that may keep the child from being confused by the "before and after" sequence of numbers. He may have learned this skill while performing the activity with the steps or strip of oil-cloth. See whether he can apply it to larger numbers.

Say something like this: "Suppose the prehistoric man has three stones in the tens-ditch and five in the ones-ditch. If he puts one more stone in the ones-ditch, how many will he have? Yes, 36. That's the next number. Take that stone out again, so there are only five in the ones-ditch again. The number is still 35. Now take another one out of the ones-ditch. What is the number now? Yes, it is 34. That's the number *before* 35." Continue with more before and after numbers.

Vary this activity by adding to or taking from the tens-ditch, or the hundreds-ditch, so the child will know which ten- and hundred-numbers come "before and after." If he seems at all confused, take him back through the steps and have more practice with this concept, until he is thoroughly familiar with the sequence.

If he enjoys doing it, go on to "two above," or "three below," and so on.

Chapter 35

COUNTING FROM 1–100
AND COUNTING BY TENS

Your child will be asked to make the numbers from 1 to 100 while he is in the first grade. Their order in this sequence may seem to vary from that in the "Prehistoric Man" presentation of the concept of ten.

Your child will probably be given a paper marked into ten columns and crossed to make ten squares. He will be asked to make a one in the upper left-hand corner, a two in the square beneath, and on down to ten. The next column begins with 11, and goes down through the teens ending with 20; the next starts with 21, and continues down through 30. Finally, in the last corner square, is 100.

Although this may appear to be confusing, it does have great value in showing the child that the idea of 1 to 10 is constant, and is in the same position in each column. It also teaches him to count by tens, and in our decimal system of mathematics, this is very important.

When the student knows his tens, he can be taught another skill. Go back to the Prehistoric Man game. Put three stones in the units-ditch and one in the tens-ditch. Ask the child to give the value of these stones; then add another stone to the tens-ditch. Ask him the value.

Continue changing the number of stones in each ditch until he can make any combinations of units and tens. This may even help him to understand the modern computers and how they work.

New methods of presenting mathematics are being introduced; even the vocabulary is changing. If he knows the basic fundamental facts of this base-ten system, he can move easily into other systems as they are called for.

Chapter 36

USING TENS IN
NUMBER COMBINATIONS

When the student knows how ten is related to all other numbers, he can use it as a base for increasing and decreasing the size of numbers. By counting by tens, he has both added and multiplied tens. He knows that if he has a certain number below ten, he can multiply it by ten by putting a "ty" on the name of the number; he can add ten, by putting a "teen" on the name. The obvious exceptions are one, two, three, and five, but they are soon understood. He can count backward by tens to subtract, and drop the "ty" to divide the multiples of ten to 100 by ten.

When your child is able to use these concepts easily and accurately, he will be happy to go on and learn his "doubles."

The "doubles" are easy because of the "odds" and "evens." From that simple beginning, he can count by "evens" and quickly discover the "doubles."

Have concrete objects at hand if he does not understand the abstractions. Say something like this: "When you know the amount made by putting two equal numbers together, you know a great deal about amounts. Doubles are the sums of two numbers that name exactly the same amount. You know that if you have one apple in one hand, and one apple in the other hand, you have two apples. Is that an odd or an even number? An even. All doubles are even numbers. Count by evens to 20: 2, 4, 6, 8, 10, 12, 14, 16, 18, 20.

"What two like-numbers can you put together to make two? 1 + 1. What twin numbers can you put together to make four? 2 + 2. To make six? eight? ten?" Go on to 20.

Write these numbers in a row on your paper and fill in the spaces between with the "doubles," thus:

1		2		4		6		8		10
	$1+1$		$2+2$		$3+3$		$4+4$		$5+5$	

10		12		14		16		18		20
	$6+6$		$7+7$		$8+8$		$9+9$		$10+10$	

Then go on: "To double numbers is fun, because it is just another form of counting. Now let's say them all to 20: $1 + 1 = 2$, $2 + 2 = 4$, and so on."

Then write the twos in the form usually given in the multiplication tables, so the child can see it more clearly.

$$1 \times 2 = 2$$
$$2 \times 2 = 4$$
$$3 \times 2 = 6$$
$$4 \times 2 = 8$$
$$5 \times 2 = 10$$
$$6 \times 2 = 12$$
$$7 \times 2 = 14$$
$$8 \times 2 = 16$$
$$9 \times 2 = 18$$
$$10 \times 2 = 20$$

Continue: "You can see that the first column on the left tells you the number of times the number is taken. The next column of numbers shows the two each time; the last column shows the answers. In counting doubles, your answer is the same as counting by twos."

Write some addition problems to show how a number can be made twice as large by *addition.*

$$\begin{array}{r} 2 \\ +2 \\ \hline 4 \end{array} \qquad 2 + 2 = 4$$

It is very important for the child to know that either way—up and down or across—is correct. He will be asked to use both methods at school.

Show the forms for multiplication.

$$\begin{array}{r} 2 \\ \times 2 \\ \hline 4 \end{array} \qquad 2 \times 2 = 4$$

Be sure that he knows, for instance, that $2 \times 4 = 8$, $4 \times 2 = 8$. Realizing that the order of the numbers in addition and multiplication does not affect the answer will always be of great value to him.

Have him look at this problem: $2 \times ? = 8$. Tell him that this is something like an algebraic equation. He must find the unknown or missing number.

Say something like this: "Count by twos and see how many numbers you say before you come to eight. Two, four, six, eight. You said four numbers—that's the answer. You multiplied two four times. If you say 2×4, your answer is eight, so that's the missing number." Give him more problems of this type, as well as more for adding and multiplication of doubles.

Show him the reverse processes: subtraction, the opposite of addition, and division, the opposite of multiplication.

The order of these numbers *is* important. They must never be changed around. The only change that can be made is in the divisor and answer. Emphasize that they may be written two ways, but the first number must always be first when using the signs.

Chapter 37

ADDING LONG COLUMNS

After the student has learned his combinations, he will get a great deal of satisfaction out of putting them to use, particularly if he can add long columns.

If he realizes that he can take out tens and mark them, he will soon be able to add any column.

Make on your paper a column of single digits, all of them 7's, 8's, and 9's. The following is an example of the problem and the solution:

Problem		Solution	
7	7	1	10
9	9	2	10
8	8	4	10
7	7	7	10
9	9		
8	8		
	48		

Say something like this: "See these numbers? Let me show you an easy way to add them. Start at the bottom. $9 + 8 = 17$. You are going to think in tens. 17 is 10 plus what number? 7." Draw a line to show that you have one ten. Now put a 7 —a very small 7— beside the number above the line, next to the 7. Say, $7 + 7 = 14$. $14 = 10 + 4$; draw a line for the ten, and put a little 4 beside the 8. $8 + 4 = 12$. Draw a line above the 8, for the 10; make a little 2 beside the 9. $9 + 2 = 11$. Draw a line for the 10, put a little 1 beside the 7. $7 + 1 = 8$. You have eight ones; now count the lines to find out how many tens there are. The bottom line doesn't count: that's part of the problem. There are one, two, three, four tens, and eight ones. The answer is 48."

Let the child practice adding a few similar columns, then show him how he can use dots instead of lines to stand for the tens; have him try keeping track of the leftover amounts in his head, not using the small numerals.

$$\begin{array}{r} 7. \\ 6 \\ 7. \\ 8. \\ 7. \\ 6. \\ \underline{9.} \\ 50 \end{array}$$

When you are sure that he understands that the lines or dots are used only when he has arrived at a ten, you may put smaller numbers in the column, pointing out that he may have several numbers before they add up to ten.

Chapter 38

COMBINATIONS WITH
ANSWERS ABOVE 10

Your child should have quite a knowledge of numbers by now. While he is still excited and proud of his ability, you should teach him combinations with answers above 10.

MATERIALS NEEDED

1. 20 birthday-candle holders.
2. 20 birthday candles.
3. A box of sand or clay into which the holders may be placed in an upright position.
4. Paper and pencil.

Birthday candles appeal to children, so this activity is usually enjoyed. Place the holders in two straight rows of ten each, and have the child insert the candles. Write $\begin{array}{r}10\\+10\end{array}$ on the paper, and ask him how many candles there are in each row; how many in two rows.

Say: "Now, take one candle away from the bottom row and I'll write $\begin{array}{r}10\\+\ 9\end{array}$ on the paper. What is the answer? Yes, it is 19.

"Take a candle from the top row and I'll write $\begin{array}{r}9\\+9\end{array}$. Since nine is one less than ten, the answer will be what? Yes, 18.

"Leave nine candles in the top row and seven in the bottom row. If that top row had ten, the answer would be easy, but there are only nine candles there. Make it ten; take one candle from the bottom row and put it with the nine. Now it's easy. How many left in the bottom row? One less than seven, that's six, so the answer is 16. $9 + 7 = 16$. The number of candles wasn't changed, you just put one more in the top row, to make ten."

Leave nine candles in the top row, and have the child work these problems:

$$
\begin{array}{cccccc}
9 & 9 & 9 & 9 & 9 & 9 \\
+6 & +8 & +2 & +5 & +4 & +3 \\
\end{array}
$$

For the first problem, have six candles in the bottom row; move one up to make ten in the top row; the number before six is five, so the answer is 15. Have the child continue the activity with each problem; repeat until you are sure that he understands.

Go on to eight candles in the top row; have him move two candles up, and make the units in the answer two less than the number added; with seven, move three up, and proceed as before. If he does this with six, also, he will learn that $6 + 4 = 10$, as well as $7 + 3$, and $8 + 2$, and vice versa. Have him put the row of nines on the bottom so that he will see that the order does not change the answer. He can write the numbers either way, too. Turn the candles, or the box around the other way and have him write the problems horizontally: $9 + 8$, and so on. Have him fill in missing numbers: $7 + ? = 16$, etc.

When he can slide easily from one method to another, you will find that he may sometimes want to add by recalling the doubles. As long as the results are accurate and he can add with speed, there should be no restrictions on techniques.

When addition combinations are secure in the child's mind, go on to subtraction. It may be that, having understood the missing-number form, he will realize that in subtraction he merely looks for the missing number. $7 + ? = 16$. $16 - 7 = 9$. It is interesting to note that when the number to be subtracted is one more than the unit number in other number, that the answer is always nine. If it is two more, the answer will be eight; $14 - 6 = 8$.

If your child has difficulty with this, take out the candles again, and say something like this: "Put 15 candles in a row—ten in one group, five in the other. I'll write *15* on the paper and put a *—6* under it. Now, it would be easy to find the answer if that were a *5* instead of a *6*. You'd know what to do—just drop the *5* off and have an answer of 10. Too bad it wasn't a 5. Let's sneak a candle away from the 10, and make the other row a 6. How many left, now? Not 10, but the number below 10; the answer is 9."

Have him count the candles, if necessary. Do several problems that have 9 for an answer: 16 — 7, 18 — 9, 17 — 8.

Go on—perhaps some other day—to subtracting nine from "teen" numbers. For 15 — 9, arrange the candles in groups of ten and five. Say: "To take away 10 would be easy; there'd be five left. To take away 9, slip one candle from the ten group; put it with the 5. The answer is 6. For 16 — 9, arrange 16 candles, 10 and 6. Take 1 away from the 10, put it with the group of six; the answer is 7." Continue until the child understands.

If you give him plenty of experience and add one concept to another gradually at this stage of his learning process, your child will be able to learn his nine-combinations for adding and subtracting and have practice in making logical choice through reasoning. When he can work successfully with nines, go on to eights, sevens, and sixes. If he knows these and his doubles, he should have no trouble adding and subtracting numbers.

Only when he is completely sure of himself and can produce accurate results should you give him a chance to add speed to these skills.

Chapter 39

HOW TO READ AND
"ROUND" LARGE NUMBERS

The child knows by now that ten is the base of all of our numbers. Have him analyze some of the bigger numbers. Have paper and pencil ready, and write this: $100 = 10 \times 10$.

Say something like this: "There are as many tens multiplied together in a number as there are zeros, or places after the first digit. 100 is 10×10, 1000 is $10 \times 10 \times 10$. This last 0 in those numbers means that there are no ones; that place is always the place to put the ones or units. The place before that tells how many tens, so that is the tens place. Before that is the place to show how many hundreds, then come thousands, tens of thousands, hundreds of thousands, then millions. A million is a thousand thousands, so you would take twice as many zeros or places as thousands: six, after you say the name *million*."

Write the number 2,345,786,201.

Say something like this: "How many units? 1. How many tens? None. How many hundreds? Two." Go through the various places to billions, then continue: "Notice the commas. Those are placed there to make the number easier to read. The first comma from the right is where you say *thousand;* the next to the left, *million;* the next, *billion*. In between the commas, you say the number just as if it were by itself. What number is before the first comma on the left? Yes, 2. Between the next two commas? Yes, 345. The next? 786. After the next one? 201. Good. Now say them again, and tell how many billions there are, how many millions, how many thousands, how many hundreds and units, how many of each group. Now read the number."

The child should say: "2 billion, 345 million, 786 thousand, two hundred and one."

Rounding the numbers should not be too difficult for him if he fully understands the "places." Say something like this: "Sometimes, when we do not need to know an exact amount, we round the number—that is, we make it a smooth, round number of 10, or multiple of 10. This usually is done with very large amounts, when there are so many things that a few more or less couldn't matter.

"If I said to you, 'How many pieces of candy did you eat?' you might not know for sure whether the answer should be 9 or 10, or possibly 11 or 12, so you would say, 'Oh, about 10.' If you knew there were more than 15, but less than 20, you might say, 'About 20.' 15 is the half-way mark between 10 and 20; the rule for rounding numbers is simple: If the amount is half-way or more than half-way between multiples of 10, go on up to the next highest one. If it's below the half-way mark, name the lower "round number." Between 100 and 200 the half way or middle point is 150. The digit 5 is the clue; 5 or above means that you go up one; below 5 means that the digit remains the same."

Write the number 2,345,786,201 again.

Continue: "Let's round this number to the nearest thousand. Which digit names the number of thousands? Yes, it is the 6. Put a dot under the 6. How many digits come after the 6? There are three. That means that your rounded number will end in three zeros. What digit is after the 6? It is a 2. Is two larger or smaller than 5? It is smaller, so leave the 6 there and add three zeros. The number 2,345,786,000 is rounded to thousands. Round the same number to the nearest hundred thousand. Which digit tells you how many hundred thousands there are? Yes, the 7. Put a dot under the 7. Your rounded number will end in how many zeros? Five. Look at the digit after the 7. It is 8. Is 8 more or less than 5? It is more, so make the 7 larger by 1; that will be 8. Add the five zeros. Your rounded number will be 2,345,800,000. Read it."

Continue this type of practice with more large numbers, until you are sure that the child understands how to "round" numbers.

Chapter 40

MORE ABOUT THE MULTIPLICATION TABLES

Perhaps your child has already learned all or part of the multiplication tables through the twelves. If he has accomplished this by rote and is sure of all of the answers, he will find any work in mathematics easier than if he did not know them. If he hasn't, then these suggested lessons will help.

"If you know the tables through the fives, and you know the nines, tens, and elevens (which are very easy), you have only 6×6, 7×7, 8×8, 6×7, 6×8, and 7×8 to learn.

"6×7 and 6×8 are not so hard. If you know $3 \times 7 = 21$, 6×7 is double that: 42. $3 \times 8 = 24$; 6×8 is double *that*. Sometimes 7×8 seems difficult. Think of it this way: $56 = 7 \times 8$; you have 5, 6, 7, 8 in a row. Try this method of learning the nines: 2×9. Drop down one from the two, and ask yourself, 'What number added to one makes nine? It is eight, so the answer is 18. 3×9. Drop down to two. What added to two makes nine? It is 7, so the answer is 27. Continue in this way through all the nines to 9×9. There is a pattern after that, too. Perhaps you can find it. The elevens are just two of each digit.

"The twelves are easy, too. $12 = 10 + 2$, so take the number to be multiplied $\times$ 10, then add the number's double. $10 + 2 = 12$, $20 + 4 = 24$ and so on: $5 \times 10 + 10 = 60$, $6 \times 10 + 12 = 72$; it must work for all the numbers to be multiplied by 12.

"There's an easy way to multiply two-place numbers by 11. Just add the digits across, and put the sum in between the digits—the tens place. $11 \times 11 = 121$, $11 \times 12 = 132$, $23 \times 11 = 253$. Perhaps you can figure out why that is true. $85 \times 11 = 935$.

$8 + 5 = 13$. You can't put both the *1* and the *3* in tens place, so put the *3* there, and add the *1* to the *8*. Try to do this with some more numbers times 11."

A knowledge of the relationships, sequences, and comparative values of the numbers found in the multiplication tables is important to the child's understanding of what he is doing when he is using them. He should be able to see whether or not answers to his problems are reasonable and in accordance with what they should be—whether or not they satisfy his own logical judgment.

Also, much pleasure can be gained by working with numbers as entities not concerned with problems, by seeing sequences, and by finding new patterns.

Have your child look at the answers to the twos through 15. Write them, or have him write them in sequence: 2, 4, 6, 8, 10, 12, 14, 16, 18, 20, 22, 24, 26, 28, 30.

Say something like this: "All of these have what kind of endings? Yes, they are even. Whenever a number ends with a 2, 4, 6, 8, or zero, you will know that its smallest factor is two—you can always divide it by two. Now look at the answers to the threes."

Write down: 3, 6, 9, 12, 15, 18, 21, 24, 27, 30, 33, 36, 39, 42, 45.

"If you were to add the digits in order to each of the answers to the twos, you would have these numbers. Try it: $2 + 1 = 3$, $4 + 2 = 6$, $6 + 3 = 9$, $8 + 4 = 12$, and so on. Some of the endings are even, some are odd—every other one, in fact.

"Add the numbers that have two digits, across. $1 + 2 = 3$, $1 + 5 = 6$, $1 + 8 = 9$. You can go on, and find that those digit sums can always be divided by three. No matter how large a number is, if its digit sum can be divided by three, the number can be divided by three. Try this number. 7752. $7 + 7 + 5 + 2 = 21$. $2 + 1 = 3$. 7752 divided by $3 = 2584$. You can always use that method to discover if a number is an even multiple of three.

"The answers to the fours are all even, too. They are, of course, double those of the twos."

Write the answers through 4×15: 4, 8, 12, 16, 20, 24, 28, 32, 36, 40, 44, 48, 52, 56, 60.

Continue: "The even endings are in this order: 4, 8, 2, 6, 0, all the way through all multiples of four. You are not sure that a number can be divided evenly by four just because the ending is even, but you do know that a number with an odd ending cannot be divided by four.

"Write down the answers for the fives, through 5 × 15. It is easy to see that any number ending in 5 or 0 can be divided evenly by five. The 5 × 2 and 5 × 3 answers are in the tens, 5 × 4 and 5 × 5 are in the twenties, 5 × 6 and 5 × 7 are in the thirties, 5 × 8 and 5 × 9 in the forties, 5 × 10 and 5 × 11 in the fifties, 5 × 12 and 5 × 13 in the sixties, 5 × 14 and 5 × 15 in the seventies, and so on. All the even numbers multiplied by five have answers ending in zero; the uneven numbers multiplied by five have answers ending in five."

Write the answers to the sixes through 15: 6, 12, 18, 24, 30, 36, 42, 48, 54, 60, 66, 72, 78, 84, 90. Then say: "These answers are all evens, too, just as the twos and fours are, only in a different sequence. How is it different? Add the digits across: $1 + 2 = 3$, $1 + 8 = 9$, and so on. Those digit sums are divisible by three, too; but that won't help you much when factoring except to tell you that if the digits add up that way, the number might be divisible by six; if they don't, you might as well not try six as a factor."

Write the answers to the sevens through × 15: 7, 14, 21, 28, 35, 42, 49, 56, 63, 70, 77, 84, 91, 98, 105.

Say something like this: "The interesting thing about those answers is that every digit is represented: 7, 4, 1, 8, 5, 2, 9, 6, 3, 0; find them in sequence and see. You know that *any* number at all *might* be divisible by 7. Add the digits across. All the digits appear there, too. Notice the pattern of decreasing odd numbers, and decreasing even numbers: 7, 5, 3, 1, 8, 6, 4, 2, and so on, in the digit sums. That won't help you find the factors of a number, but it *is* a pattern.

"Remember—you can tell about the factors of 2, 5, and 10 at a glance. You can be sure of three if the digit sums are three and nine. If the numbers are even and the digits add across to three, you can *try* 6. If the numbers are even, you can try 4 and 8.

"With any number, you can take a chance on 7 and 11—if the number is above 6."

Chapter 41

NUMBER SEQUENCES

Number sequences are interesting to children. The basic patterns help them to understand the four basic processes. The relationships between numbers is so vital to mathematics that the sooner your child acquires a "feel" for them, the better student he will be.

Start by showing him a simple sequence, counting by twos, with one part missing. As in reading or listening, he is asked to anticipate what comes next, by the logic and sequence of what came before. Write this sequence on paper: 2, 4, 6, 8, ——.

Say something like this: "There is a space, here, for you to fill in. Read the numbers aloud. Start at the left, 2, 4, 6, 8; what comes next? 10. You know that, don't you? These are all even numbers, starting with the lowest even number, so, of course, you can't miss. Look at this sequence. 1, 3, 5, 7, ——. What is the next number? Yes, 9. What kind of numbers are in the sequence? Odd. Now look at this sequence: 15, 13, 11, 9, ——5. Can you find the missing number? What's different about that sequence? Yes, it's going down, the numbers are growing smaller. What two things can you do when you have to make a number less? You can subtract, or divide."

Draw curves between the numbers in this way:

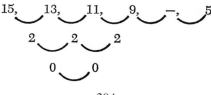

Continue: "How much does the 15 go down to reach 13? That's right, 2. $13 - 2 = 11$, $11 - 2 = 9$, $9 - 2 = 7$. The next number must be seven, to follow the same pattern. Does $7 - 2 = 5$? Yes, so you know that the answer is correct."

Show the student a multiplication sequence:

$$3, \quad 6, \quad 12, \quad —.$$

Say something like this: "Do these numbers go up or down? Yes, up. Do they increase by the same amount? Try it and see. $3 + 3 = 6$, but $6 + 3$ does not equal 12. Addition doesn't work, so we must try multiplication. $3 \times 2 = 6$, $6 \times 2 = 12$. That's right, so the next number should be 24. Here again, if you make the curves, the numbers below them will cancel out."

Write the following sequence:

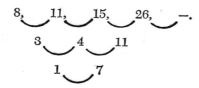

Then say: "Look at these numbers. They do not form a sequential pattern since the numbers below the curve do not cancel out. Therefore, with most numbers it is best to check the accuracy of the pattern before deciding on the answer, because there may not be a pattern."

You can use the same technique with division sequences. Write these numbers on paper: 18, 9;   8, 4;   —, 3.

Say something like this: "These numbers go down, so try subtraction first. The differences are not the same. Try division. $18 \div 9 = 2$; $8 \div 4 = 2$. That's correct so far. What divided by 2 is 3? The missing number must be 6. Put the curve beneath the numbers, between 18 and 9, 8 and 4, 6 and 3. The 2's cancel out to zero.

Mix two concepts of increasing and decreasing values:

$$2, \quad 7, \quad 12, \quad 17, \quad 14, \quad 11, \quad \underline{\quad}$$

Say: "Part of this sequence goes up, the other part down.

$$7 - 2 = 5; \quad 12 - 7 = 5; \quad 17 - 12 = 5;$$
$$17 - 14 = 3; \quad 14 - 11 = 3; \quad 11 - 3 = 8.$$

The missing number must be 8. Put the differences, 5, 5, 5, 3, 3, 3, below the curves; they cancel out to zero, so the answer must be correct."

From this type of sequence, the child will receive practice in visual acuity; he will realize that the pattern may vary but still retain a balance since there is the same number of equal values on each side.

There is a special sequence in which children usually have great interest. It is one bound closely to nature and to our heritage from the ancient Greeks; it is called the Golden Section, and it was used for producing harmony of proportion in architecture and other arts. Make a copy of this for the child to examine:

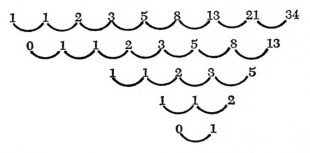

This sequence of numbers can be continued indefinitely by adding each number to the one preceding it.

Say something like this: "Notice that, as you subtract one number from another sequentially, the differences repeat the sequences: 1, 1, 2, 3 and so on. When this happens, you know you have the sequence called the Golden Section. Add the numbers as you read them across: $1 + 1 = 2$. $1 + 2 = 3$. $2 + 3 = 5$. Now go right on to the end."

There are other numbers that can be discovered. The sums of the numbers below and to the right of each number equal the following number. The sum of the numbers along the right edge of the pattern, $1 + 2 + 5 + 13$ equals the last number but one.

It might amuse the child to have him draw dots on lines on his paper to match the numbers in the Golden Section. He can find a similar pattern in pine cones, flowers, and leaves.

Chapter 42

TERMS USED IN PROCESSES
AND STORY PROBLEMS

There are four processes by which quantities can be "reckoned." The child should know and understand the terms that apply to these processes. While explaining the terms, have a piece of paper and pencil at hand.

Write down the key words and numbers found here as you explain them, so the child can see them and learn to say and make them. If the words seem difficult for him, write them in syllables, have him say and spell them one syllable at a time—as, for example, *com-mu-ta-tive.*

A child is very likely to find the facts interesting and retain many of them if they are presented clearly and deliberately enough for him to absorb them.

Say something like this: "The word *add* comes from the Latin word *addere,* meaning to unite or join. When we add, we join numbers and increase their values, their quantities. *Quantum* in Latin means *how much* or *how many,* so *quantity* means just how much or how many a certain number stands for.

"*Multiply*—from the Latin *multus* meaning *much* or *many*—also tells us to increase the quantity of a number. Actually, multiplying is a short way to add. It is easier to multiply by one number than to add a long column of repeated numbers.

"Both addition and multiplication increase the quantity expressed by a number. The numbers to be added or multiplied can be in any order. They are *commutative. Commutative* is from the Latin *con,* meaning *with,* and *mutans,* meaning *changing.* The numbers in addition and multiplication can change places with each other and the answer will be the same. For instance, $3 + 2 = 5$ and $2 + 3 = 5$; $6 \times 5 = 30$ and $5 \times 6 = 30$. The order doesn't matter. This is true of any other numbers ever used in addition or multiplication.

"Subtraction, from the Latin *subtractus,* meaning *carried away,* does just that—carries away a part of the base number, the number with which we start, leaving the quantity less.

"Divide, from the Latin *dividere,* meaning *to force asunder* or *to part,* here means to separate into parts." (It is important for the child to know what division does to a certain base number: that it divides it into the number of parts named by the divisor, and that sometimes there is an amount left over—a number of units that are a part of the base number. These were not divided; they still remain undivided, so they are called the "remainder").

Continue: "The answer in division is bound to be smaller than the base, and, of course, the remainder also is smaller than the base." (The child has learned this with smaller numbers; have him relate the concept with larger ones.)

"The answer in both subtraction and division will be smaller than the number with which you start. The processes of subtraction and division are *noncommutative.* The numbers used have to stay in a specified order." (The words used to indicate that subtraction or division must be employed should be understood. The child should know that "four less two" and "two from four" mean the same thing; that this is true of "six divided by three" and "three taken into six." Problems should always be rephrased until the proper order is known. The first number to appear in a problem is not always the base.)

The child should know the meaning of a few more terms used in relation to the processes.

He must be able to identify the base numbers in each problem he has to solve—the numbers with which he begins each process.

Say something like this, using numbers as illustrations: "*End* or *and* are endings sometimes added to verbs to form nouns. When we add, we have to have "things" to add—in this case, numbers. We call the numbers we add *addends.*

"The base number from which we subtract another number is called a *subtrahend.* That's easier to say than 'subtractend.' The number we subtract from the subtrahend is called a *minuend.*

Minuend is from a Latin word *minuere* meaning to make smaller. *Minute* is a small amount of time; *diminish* means to make *smaller; minuend* is a number that will make the *subtrahend* smaller.

"In multiplication, the base number is the *multiplicand,* and in division it is the *dividend.* The endings *er* and *or* are often added to verbs to name that which applies to the performer of the action indicated by the verb. The number by which the *dividend* is divided is called the *divisor,* the number by which the *multiplicand* is multiplied is the *multiplier.*"

The name of the answers resulting from each process must be known, also. Often problems indicate the process to be used, by calling for the answers by their specific names.

Say something like this: "There is a Latin word *summa* which means the *highest point.* We speak of the summit of a mountain; that's the top, the highest part. When we add the answer, the total will be the highest amount, the greatest quantity or number, so we call it the *sum.* The sum of anything is larger than any of the parts, or addends. *Product* is something produced or made. If you multiply one number by another you produce a new number. The Latin *pro* means *for* or *before, ducere* means *lead* or *bring. Product* in our language means a thing *brought forth;* so when we bring forth a new number by multiplying, we call it a *product.*

"In subtraction, the answer is called the *difference.* We find the difference in quantity between two numbers. In division the answer is the *quotient.* The Latin *quot* means *how many.* The ending *ent* makes the word a noun. The *i* is put in to make it easier to say. A quotient tells how many times one number is contained in another."

The vocabulary used in "story" problems can be confusing to a child. He should be shown how to rephrase or paraphrase these problems—to say them in his own words in different ways until he can find the base numbers.

He should know what terms call for addition. They might be *add; find the total or sum; how many in all; how much altogether; combine; increased by.*

He should discover whether the base numbers can be used better as addends or as multiplicands. The expressions that indicate multiplication are often *multiplied by; times as much, or many; find the product.*

Subtraction, which is the reverse or opposite of addition, could be indicated by: *find the difference; subtract; take away, or take from; less; how much or how many less; more than, greater than, less than; increased by or decreased by how much or how many; remained; left over.*

For division, the reverse or opposite of multiplication, the terms might be: *find the quotient; divided by; how many times as much; contained in; taken into.*

In order to find his way around in an arithmetic book or any mathematics book, a student must know the meaning of the words and terms used in reference to numbers, not vaguely, but with certainty. Go over some of these again to make sure that he knows them. Write examples as you explain the terms used in the processes. Have your child write them, spell them correctly, and write more examples of each.

Say something like this:

> "A 5, or a 6, or a 27—any of the number of things from zero to infinity—are designated by different names according to their use or needs.
>
> "1.   As one of the various symbols, they are *numerals.* 2, two, II.
>
> "2.   As specific shapes, the Arabic figures are *digits.* 0, 1, 2, 3, 4, 5, 6, 7, 8, 9.
>
> "3.   As amounts, they are *numbers*—counting numbers. This does not include zero.
>
> "4.   As unbroken, complete entities, they are *whole numbers,* or *integers.* 8, 35, etc.
>
> "5.   If they are divisible by two, they are *even numbers;* if not, they are *odd numbers.*
>
> "6.   If they can be divided only by themselves and one, they are *prime* numbers.
>
> "7.   A product of two or more numbers is a *multitple.* $2 \times 3 = 6.$
>
> "8.   As one of the numbers multiplied by another to produce a multiple, they are *factors.* 2 and 3 are factors of 6.
>
> "9.   A number that can be divided by more than one factor is a *common multiple* of those factors. 6 is common to 2, 3, 6, 1.
>
> "10.   A factor that is contained evenly in different multiples is a *common factor* of those multiples. $2 \times 3 = 6;$ $9 \times 3 = 27.$ 3 is common to 6 and 27.
>
> "11.   A *rational* number is any number that can be expressed as a quotient of two integers, not zero."

When a child realizes that arithmetic is a matter of making logical choices, his battle is half over.

After he has absorbed these terms, have him read a story problem. Discuss the meaning with him. Say something like this: "What do you want to find out; is it an amount of dollars, a number of people, the size of something?

"What is the *base* number or numbers given? What do you already know?

"Is there more than one part, one step?

"Which is the first, the basic step?

"Should the answer be larger than the base number or smaller?

"If larger, can you find the answer by adding some numbers, or is it simpler to multiply; does it increase over and over again?

"If smaller, can you subtract one number from another? Or is it getting smaller over and over again; should it be divided?"

Have the child ask himself such questions about each step.

After he has performed the necessary processes and has arrived at an answer, have him go back and rephrase the problem again, putting the answer where the "unknown" or missing fact was before. He should then ask himself, "Does that sound reasonable? Does it make sense?"

Chapter 43

ANALYSIS OF NUMBERS:
THE FOUR PROCESSES WITH
LARGER NUMBERS

The child has now learned simple addition and multiplication, and their reverse processes of subtraction and division.

Since our numbers are arranged around the ten base, your child should think of them in relation to ten and be able to analyze them.

MATERIALS NEEDED

1. Paper and pencils.
2. A box of toothpicks.

Ask the child to count out ten toothpicks and put them in a pile, then place a single toothpick to one side. Write on the paper: $10 + 1 = 11$. Have him continue working with the toothpicks and writing; go on with $10 + 2 = 12$, and so on, until he has seen the value of all of the teens in relation to ten; then have him make two piles of ten and continue through the twenties, writing $10 + 10 = 20$; $10 + 10 + 1 = 21$; $10 + 10 + 2 = 22$; and so on, to 100.

Each number need not be done in sequence; skip some, as the activity could become tiresome. Ask him to represent certain numbers by using the toothpicks, then write the analysis on his paper. Show him how to write them in shorter forms; for instance $2(10) + 3 = 23$. Explain that the parentheses, the curved lines around numbers, mean *multiply* or *times*, just as the $\times$ sign does.

This analysis should help the child to understand "carrying" and "borrowing."

Give him the problem 28 + 36. Have him put the addends down, one above the other, then make two piles of ten toothpicks, and one of eight; three piles of ten and one of six. Tell him to put the pile of eight and the pile of six together and count them.

Say something like this: "There are 14, so take ten and place those over with the piles of tens. Put the number four down on the paper under the numbers that show the ones, under the eight and six. Now, how many piles of ten are there? There are six, counting the pile you carried over. Put a little *1* over that tens column in your problem, to show that you add it in with the other tens. Your answer is 64."

Have the child perform this activity with a few more numbers. After he has learned to do it with his hands, and visually with his eyes, combining them with his thinking processes, he should be able to remember how to do it by thinking and writing only, and perhaps by thinking alone.

Analyze some larger numbers. It would take a long time to count out hundreds of toothpicks, so just let him make a large pile of them represent 100. Then write some more analyses, as $235 = 2(100) + 3(10) + 5$, and $876 = 8(100) + 7(10) + 6$. Emphasize the fact that what is on one side of an equal sign must always have exactly the same value as that on the other side. Be sure that he "carries" the piles of 10 and 100 over to the tens and hundreds groups, and at the same time puts the number above the ten and hundred columns in the problem, when he adds 235 and 876.

Have him reverse the order of the numbers and add 876 and 235, to prove that the sequence of the number does not matter in addition.

Proceed to subtraction. Take the two numbers 36 and 28 again. Have him arrange the piles as he did before. Ask him: "Could you take the number in that pile of 30 + 6 away from the pile of 20 + 8? No, of course not. There's not enough in the second pile."

After he has seen this, ask him if he could take as many as there are in the 28-pile away from the 36. Write the problem, with the 28 under 36. First he will have to take the eight from the six. He will see that this can't be done, so tell him he can borrow a pile of tens from the group of three tens. He can then take eight away from 10 + 6, and will have and leave eight. Have him write an 8 in the ones column in the problem under the 6 and 8; then cross out the 3, putting a 2 above it to show that there are only two tens there now. When he takes the two tens away, there will be no number to put in the tens place. This same activity can be performed with other problems, some in the hundreds, if he needs the added demonstration.

The same analysis of numbers can be used to show how to carry tens and hundreds in multiplication. Write the problem, 28×3 on the paper, one number above the others. Make piles of toothpicks for $2(10) + 8$.

Say something like this: "If you multiply by three, how many groups of piles like this will you have to have? Yes, three. We won't make that many piles, we'll just multiply. First, what is 3×8? Yes, 24. If you are not sure, make three piles of 8 and count them. You can put only units in the ones columns, so take the four ones away from the $20 + 4$. How many tens left? Yes, two. Put the two above the 2 in the tens column. Now look at the tens piles again. How many are there? Yes, two. Now, $3 \times 2 = 6$. If you make another set of two piles of tens, and then another one, that will be six piles. But there are two more piles you had to carry over; you'll have to add those to the 6, and put an 8 in your answer, under the tens columns. Your answer is 84."

Do this with a few more problems until he seems to understand them.

For those who are learning two-place multiplication, start out with some simple problems, so that they can learn the pattern. Write 28 and 23, in the correct form for multiplication, one above the other.

Make some piles for 28: $2(10) + 8$.

Say something like this: "28 has to be taken 23 times. We wouldn't want to write 28 down 23 times, so we'll multiply. Since 23 is $2(10) + 3$, we can multiply by 3 first; that's easy. $3 \times 8 = 24$; put the 4 in the ones place, carry the 2. $30 \times 2 = 60$; that's six tens. Add the number of tens you carried, and put the 8 in the tens place. Now you have to multiply by the two tens in the 23. That means that the answer will have to be put in the tens column; that's over there, under the 8 in 84, because 84 is eight tens plus four ones. $2 \times 8 = 16$. Put the 6 in the tens column, and place a little 1 up there above the 2 you carried before; you may cross that 2 out if it bothers you. $2 \times 2 = 4$, add that 1—that'll be five—

and put the 5 before the 6. Add the two answers, and you will have 644. Remember that is really $6(100) + 4(10) + 4$, so the answer is 644. Sometimes it helps to put a zero in the ones place in the second number of the answer."

Remind the child again that to the extreme right is the place for single units, for ones; to the left of that is the tens place; then comes the hundreds place, and so on.

For division, write the problem down in this form: $2\overline{)28}$. Make piles of two tens and eight units for 28. Say something like this: "If you separate those piles of 20 into two parts, how many piles will you have? That's right, two. In division, you must know how many are in each pile after you have separated them. How many tens are there in each pile? Yes, one ten. In all the other processes —addition, multiplication, and subtraction—you always wrote down the numbers in ones place first. In division, you start at the other end. In this problem, you put the first answer in the tens place. Put the *1* over the *2* in the dividend. That's one ten. Now look at the pile of eight units; divide that into two parts. How many in each part? Yes, four. Put *4* in the ones place in your quotient."

Write the problem: $2\overline{)38}$.

Say something like this: "$38 = 3(10) + 8$. Make the piles. First divide the tens by two. Now how many in each pile? Yes, there are 15. How many tens in each part? Just one, and five units left over. Put the *1* above the *3*, in your problem; that is one ten. Now you have some left over in the piles that have not been divided; how many altogether? Ten. You'll have to add that to the pile of eight, and divide by two. Make two equal piles out of 18, and how many are there in each pile? Yes, nine. Put a 9 in your answer in the ones' place; your answer is 19, which is one ten plus eight ones."

After this idea has been demonstrated once, the child should be able to see that the number left over is the number of tens that must be added to the units remaining to be divided.

With two-place divisors, try this method:

$$12\overline{)384}$$

Write the above problem on your paper, and say something like this: "Since you may not know the multiplication tables of twelves, you might not know how many times 12 is contained in 384. Draw a circle around the first number in the divisor. Can you divide one into three? Yes, so draw a circle around the 3. Now, you are still dividing by 12, so actually you are finding out how many times 12 is contained in 38; the answer then will have to be written above the 8. Put a little dot over the 8, above the line and over any other numbers following 8, so you will remember where to put your answer.

"Say, one into three is three; put the 3 where the first dot is." Go on with the rest of the problem, being sure that he divides, multiplies, subtracts, checks the remainder to see that it isn't more than the divisor, brings down the next number, divides, and so on. Using squared paper is a big help in dividing the large numbers; it avoids the possibility of confusing the numbers.

When the numbers to be divided become larger and "trial" answers have to be found, there is an easier way to divide.

With this method, no trial quotient can be too small. It should never be too large, so the safest thing for a child to do is to choose one that he knows very well is too small.

Copy this problem on a sheet of paper and then write the solution:

Problem	Solution
$75\overline{)6835}$	$75\overline{)6835}$ 40
	3000
	3835 50
	3750
Answer	85 1
	75
91 R 10	10 91
$75\overline{)6835}$	

First, have the child determine which part of the dividend should be used. He should say: "75 is not contained in 68, so I'll have to say 75 into 683. This means the answer would start at the 3 in the tens place, so I'll put one zero to the right of that right hand space. I can put any number before the zero, so I'll just write 4; that should be small enough. Then 40 times 75 equals 3000. I'll put that under the 6835 and subtract. Next I'll put 50 at the right. That should be a small enough number. 50 × 75 = 3750. I'll put that under the 3835, and subtract. The remainder is 75. 75 is contained in 85 only once, so that 1 will belong in the ones' place; I won't need a zero. Now, I'll add all of the answers. The sum is 91. I'll subtract the 75 from 85; the remainder is 10. My quotient is 91, with a remainder of 10."

The child should know how to prove that his answers are correct. Since division is a process that is the reverse of multiplication, proof can be established by using the reverse process, that of multiplication.

If he multiplies the divisor by the quotient and adds the remainder, the answer should be the dividend. $75 \times 91 = 6825$; 6825 plus the remainder 10 is 6835.

Have him divide more numbers by this method, until it becomes familiar to him.

To prove a multiplication problem, use the opposite process, division. An opposite or reverse method is usually called the *inverse* process, which means opposite or turned around. $6 \times 2 = 12$. $12 \div 2 = 6$. It is also true to say $12 \div 6 = 2$. This idea will help your child to understand the formulas that are sometimes used for solving percentage problems.

Chapter 44

FACTORING

Your child may know how to factor by this time. If he does not, go over this activity with him.

Refer to the section on the multiplication tables for help in factoring.

Have paper and pencil ready; if your child does not fully understand the concepts of multiplication and division, have the toothpicks at hand for further demonstration. Follow the same pattern as before: Separate the toothpicks into groups and groups of groups, as needed.

Say something like this: "In science class, you learn that elements are the parts that, when put together, produce a certain kind of thing. In mathematics, these elements, when multiplied together, are called *factors*. They can be any whole numbers, except zero. What are the factors of one? One and one. Of two? One and two. Of three? One and three. Of four? One, four and two. $2 \times 2 = 4$, so two is a factor." Go on through ten, and beyond to some larger numbers, such as the answers to the multiplication tables.

To find the smallest factors, show him this method:

Write the number 64. Say something like this: "This is an even number, so you can divide by two. The answer is even, so can you divide by two again? Yes. The answer is even, so divide by two again. Keep on until you can divide no more. Now how many twos are there? Yes, there are 6. The factors are $2 \times 2 \times 2 \times 2 \times 2 \times 2$. The 1 doesn't count, it isn't necessary as a factor as it will not change the value. You can put a little 6 above and to the right of the 2, to stand for the six times you multiply the two. A number placed that way is called an *exponent*. All you have to remember about it now is that it means the number of times a number is multiplied by itself."

Show him the solution on his paper:

$$
\begin{array}{r}
2)\,64 \\
2)\overline{32} \\
2)\overline{16} \\
2)\overline{8} \\
2)\overline{4} \\
2)\overline{2} \\
\hline
1
\end{array}
$$

Write this number: 2343. Say: "Can you divide that number by 2? No, it isn't even. Try 3. In the section on the multiplication tables, you remember, you learned how to test a number to see if it is divisible by 3. Add the digits, across: $2 + 3 + 4 + 3 = 12$; $1 + 2 = 3$. 3 is divisible by 3, so you can use 3 for the first factor of 2343. 2343 divided by $3 = 781$. 2 won't do, 3 won't do." Use some of the ideas given elsewhere for finding even divisors. You will come to 11, and can complete the factoring.

$$
\begin{array}{r}
3)\,2343 \\
11)\overline{781} \\
\hline
71
\end{array}
$$

The factors are 3, 11, 71.

"The numbers you have factored do not have a common factor; the last group of factors cannot be written with an exponent, because there are not two or more of the same factor."

This is one way to find the least common multiple of a group of numbers. Write the numbers 6, 9, 4. The child may know his "tables" well enough to know right away that, in this case, the least common multiple is 36. If he does not, or if the numbers presented are more difficult, tell him to find the largest number and check to see if it can be divided evenly by both four and six. It can't, so he should multiply the 9 by 2. 18 is all right for 6, but not for 4. Multiply 9 by 3. Continue in sequence with 4. That will do, so 36 is the least common multiple. If it had not been the correct number, the child should continue with 5, 6, and on up until he reaches a satisfactory product. This is a useful method for him to use when he is finding common denominators for adding and subtracting fractions.

Chapter 45

FRACTIONS AND DECIMALS

The whole area of fractions and decimals in the general field of mathematics is one that your child will be studying throughout his academic career.

As soon as he has mastered the basic fundamentals of the four processes—or whenever you feel he is sufficiently advanced and interested—you should help him to learn the first general principles.

The following is a suggested outline of a short course to whet his appetite in both areas.

Say something like this: "A *fraction* is a part of a whole. The word is from the Latin *frangere*, meaning *to break*. If an integer is broken into parts, it becomes a group of fragments, each fragment being a fraction of the whole. When writing simple fractions, the numeral telling the size of the parts is placed below a line, as ⅓. The number of parts is shown above that line. If two thirds are named, the fraction is written as ⅔.

"The number below the line, denoting the size of the parts, is called the *denominator*. *De* means *of*, *nom* means *name*, so denominator is the *name of* the size; 3, called *thirds* in fractions, tells the size of the part of a whole thing. The number above the line names the number of parts; it is called the *numerator*—something like numeral, it means the amount, the quantity of parts. There are two thirds in that fraction."

Make some number lines like this on your paper. The child may make more if he has a ruler. The size of the divisions are not important, but there must be ten parts, as shown below.

```
0    1    2    3    4    5    6    7    8    9    10
```

Say something like this: "Each space on the line represents one whole. The line is marked to show two wholes, three wholes, and so on. Between *0* and *1* are all the fractions—all amounts less than 1. There are as many fractions as there are numbers, and their possible divisors reach to infinity, farther than you can even think about. There are innumerable fractions that you'll never have to deal with; there are a few that you must know. There is ½. On one of the lines that you have made, make little marks to show one half of each space. You could use other number lines like this to show thirds, fourths, fifths, sixths, and so on. It would be pretty hard to divide that short space into anything beyond eighths, but you can imagine the larger fractions. Notice that when the numerator and denominator become the same, it's always one whole. Remember that $\frac{2}{2}$, $\frac{5}{5}$, $\frac{55}{55}$, $\frac{100}{100}$, or any fraction like that always equals one.

"When the numerator is smaller than the denominator, the fraction is proper—the simplest kind of fraction.

"Between *2* and *3*, on the number line, there are the same fractions as between *0* and *1*. This is equally true of the spaces between any other two *consecutive* numbers.

"Consecutive means one right after the other in direct sequential order. When, on the number line, we reach the *half* between *1* and *2*, we have arrived at $1 + \frac{1}{2}$. We write this $1\frac{1}{2}$. It means one whole and a half of one whole. We might have $25 + \frac{3}{4}$ ($25\frac{3}{4}$), or $136 + \frac{11}{16}$ ($136\frac{11}{16}$)—any possible combinations of whole numbers and fractions. These are called *mixed numbers*. They are a mixture of the two forms—whole numbers and fractions.

"$2\frac{1}{2}$ is made up of four halves plus one half, or five halves. $2\frac{1}{2} = \frac{5}{2}$. Look at the number line and see if this isn't true.

"*To change mixed numbers to improper fractions, multiply the whole number by the denominator, and add the numerator.*

"A fraction with a numerator larger than the denominator is

called an improper fraction; for answers to problems, an improper fraction usually has to be changed to a mixed number.

"Count the five halves again. How many whole numbers do they make? Yes, two plus one half.

"*To change an improper fraction to a mixed number, divide the numerator by the denominator,* and make a fraction with the remainder as the numerator; the denominator with which you divided will still be the denominator."

Have the child perform these operations with more mixed numbers and improper fractions. Have him check on the line, to see that some improper fractions equal whole numbers: $\frac{4}{2}$, $\frac{6}{3}$, $\frac{8}{4}$, etc.

"There are fractions that can be reduced to simpler form. $\frac{1}{4}$ is in as simple a form as it can be, but $\frac{2}{4}$ is not. Two and four have a common factor, two. Divide both the numerator and denominator by two. Remember, if you do the same thing by division or multiplication to both parts of a fraction, you do not change its value. $\frac{2}{4} = \frac{1}{2}$. Look at the number lines to see if this is true. In fact, $\frac{4}{8}$, $\frac{3}{6}$, and $\frac{2}{4}$ all equal $\frac{1}{2}$. This is true of $\frac{5}{10}$, $\frac{6}{12}$, $\frac{7}{14}$, $\frac{8}{16}$, $\frac{9}{18}$, $\frac{10}{20}$, and any other fractions whose numerator is half of its denominator.

"Reduce these fractions: $\frac{3}{9}$, $\frac{6}{8}$, $\frac{20}{25}$. Divide by the common factors, 3, 2, 5. If you could check these on a line, you would find that the reduced fractions are equal to the ones that were reduced. See how important it is to know how to factor.

"You cannot add or subtract fractions unless they have the same denominators. It is easy to add fractions such as $\frac{1}{5}$, $\frac{2}{5}$ and $\frac{3}{5}$. You want to know the number of fifths, so you add one, two, and three. That makes $\frac{6}{5}$ or $1\frac{1}{5}$.

"But you can't add $\frac{1}{2}$ and $\frac{1}{3}$ that easily. You know you can't add one dog and one book. You can add only things of the same name or denomination. You can add fractions only if they have the same denominator. What number is a multiple of both 2 and 3? 6, of course.

$$\frac{1}{2} + \frac{1}{3} = \frac{3}{6} + \frac{2}{6} = \frac{5}{6}."$$

Write the problem: $8\frac{7}{9} + 3\frac{5}{12}$. Tell the child to find the common denominators as he was told earlier. To find a common multiple, he must divide, then multiply. Then have him write the problem like this:

$$8 \frac{7}{9} = 8 \frac{}{36}$$

$$3 \frac{5}{12} = 3 \frac{}{36}$$

When he has found the answer, $11^{43}\!/_{36}$, he must know that it means $11 + {}^{43}\!/_{36}$ or $11 + 1 + {}^7\!/_{36}$, which is $12^7\!/_{36}$. Have him subtract fractions that will require borrowing.

Write this problem:

$$4\frac{1}{3} = 4^4\!/_{12}$$
$$-2\frac{3}{4} = 2^9\!/_{12}$$

Say something like this: "You can't take 9 from 4, so you'll have to borrow from the whole number. One whole is how many twelfths? Yes, it's $^{12}\!/_{12}$. You have borrowed 12 twelfths, which added to 4 twelfths makes 16 twelfths. Now the problem is this:

$$3^{16}\!/_{12}$$
$$\underline{-2^9\!/_{12}}$$

That's easy to subtract. The answer is $1^7\!/_{12}$. Always remember that the number you add to the numerator when you have to borrow is the same number as the denominator of the fractions you are subtracting. In this case it was 12.

"To multiply by a fraction, you do the same thing that you do when you take a fractional part of a number. Multiplication is a commutative process, so the order of the numbers can be changed. You can say $\frac{1}{3}$ of 9 or $9 \times \frac{1}{3}$. They mean the same thing. Check the line that you have divided into thirds, and check this: $\frac{1}{3}$ of $\frac{1}{2} = \frac{1}{6}$. Now find $\frac{1}{2}$ of $\frac{1}{3}$. They are the same, aren't they? The same thing is true of all fractions that are multiplied.

"Now find $\frac{1}{3}$ of nine. It is 3. Write this $9 \times \frac{1}{3}$. It should have the same answer: 3. You could write the problem like this: $\frac{9}{1} \times \frac{1}{3}$, then say $9 \times 1 = 9$. $3 \times 1 = 3$. Your answer is $\frac{9}{3} = 3$. All the numerators in a fraction multiplication problem must be multiplied by each other, and all the numbers in the denominators must be multiplied also. Your answer will be another fraction, which can be reduced, if necessary, to a mixed number, a whole number, or a lower form of the same fraction."

Write down some more fractions and have the child multiply them. Give him some mixed numbers to change to improper fractions, before multiplying, as

$$4\frac{1}{3} \times 6\frac{1}{2} = \frac{13}{3} \times \frac{13}{2} = \frac{169}{6} = 28\frac{1}{6}$$

Write this problem on the paper: $9 \div \frac{1}{3}$

Say something like this: "You know that division is the *inverse* process of multiplication, the opposite. Instead of dividing the nine by three, you multiply it. You can never change the order in a division problem. If $\frac{1}{3}$ is the divisor, it remains the divisor. In this problem, you must divide by $\frac{1}{3}$.

"Look at the number line again. Find the number 9. There are nine spaces, representing 9. Each of those spaces must be divided by $\frac{1}{3}$. How many thirds in one space? Yes, there are three. How many in nine spaces? 3×9, or 27. You can see why you must multiply by the denominator of the fraction; that tells the parts into which one has been divided. When you multiply that by the number to be divided, you will know the total amount, or the quotient. Now, suppose you had to divide 9 by $\frac{2}{3}$. Look at the number line again. There are only half as many parts that are two thirds long, so you'll have to divide the 27 by 2. The answer is $13\frac{1}{2}$.

"*To divide by a fraction, multiply by the denominator, and divide by the numerator.*

"The easiest way to do this is to invert the fraction by which you are dividing—turn it upside down, then multiply.

$$\frac{9}{1} \times \frac{3}{2} = \frac{27}{2} = 13\frac{1}{2}$$

"Try some more.

$$\frac{2}{3} \div \frac{1}{2} = \frac{2}{3} \times \frac{2}{1} = \frac{4}{3} = 1\frac{1}{3}$$
$$2\frac{1}{2} \div 3\frac{1}{3} = \frac{5}{2} \div \frac{10}{3} = \frac{5}{2} \times \frac{3}{10} = \frac{15}{20} = \frac{3}{4}$$

"You could have canceled in that problem. Any number above the line and any number below the line that have common factors can be divided by those factors. You could put all the numerators above one line if you wanted to, and all the denominators below the line. They mean the same thing either way. The numerator 5, and the denominator 10, have a common factor, two. Five into five is one; five into ten is two. Multiply the numerators, then the denominators that are not canceled, and the answer is $\frac{3}{4}$."

When your child is required to work with decimals, be sure that he knows these facts:

1. A decimal is one of the fractions that appear between the *0* and the *1* on the number line previously studied.

2. Written as a simple fraction, a decimal fraction would always have ten or some unit multiple of ten as its denominator. (The Latin word *decem* means *ten*, so this is easy to remember.)

3. A point takes the place of the denominator. $\frac{1}{10} = .1$

4. The number of "places" after the decimal point is the same as the number of zeros in the "denominator."

5. A mixed decimal is the same as a mixed number—a whole number plus a fractional part of the number one.

6. To add and subtract decimals is an easy process, because if you put the decimal points under each other, you already have the common denominator.

In $6.2 + .03 + .001$, 1000 is the common denominator; 10 and 100 both will "go into" 1000. Write the problem like this:

$$
\begin{array}{r}
6.200 \\
.030 \\
.001 \\
\hline
6.231
\end{array}
$$

You do not need to fill in the spaces with zeros, as:

$$\frac{200}{1000} = \frac{2}{10}$$

7. To multiply a number by ten, add one zero; to multiply a number by 100, add two zeros, and so on. The same number of zeros as there are in the multiplier must be added. $2 \times 10 = 20$. $2 \times 100 = 200$.

8. To divide by ten, point off one decimal place; to divide by 100, point off two places—the same number of places as there are zeros.

$$2 \div 10 = .2, \qquad 2 \div 100 = .02$$

9. To multiply a decimal by ten, move the point one place to the right; the value is increasing. To multiply a decimal by 100, move the point another place to the right; the value must be ten times as great.

10. To divide a decimal by ten, move the point one place to the left; the value must be smaller. To divide by 100, move the point two places to the left, and so on, according to the number of zeros on the end of the divisor.

11. To divide a decimal by a whole number, you just divide as usual, and put the decimal point in the quotient above the one in the dividend.

$$\begin{array}{r} .1 \\ 2\overline{).2} \end{array}$$

12. To divide a decimal by a whole number, you will have to make the divisor a whole number. You can do this by multiplying it by whatever number tells the name of its "denominator," but you'll have to do the same thing to the dividend. Remember the rule in fractions: If you divide or multiply both the numerator and the denominator by the same number, you do not change its value.

$$.4 \div .2 = \frac{.4}{.2} \qquad \frac{.4 \times 10 = 4}{.2 \times 10 = 2} = 2$$

What you did was to move the decimal point in the divisor to the end of the number, then move the decimal point in the dividend the same number of places; then you have a whole number by which you can divide, and the problem is exactly like the ones you did before. A decimal after a whole number means nothing. $2. = 2$

13. To multiply two fractions you multiply the numerators, then the denominators.

$$\tfrac{1}{10} \times \tfrac{1}{10} = \tfrac{1}{100}; \qquad \tfrac{101}{100} \times \tfrac{2}{10} = \tfrac{202}{1000}$$

It is the same with decimals.

$$.1 \times .1 = .01, \qquad 1.01 \times .2 = .202$$

When you multiply decimals, always add the number of decimal places in both multipliers to find the number of places in the product.

Chapter 46

RATIO, PERCENTAGE
AND AVERAGE

Ratio is the relation of two numbers, one to the other, in respect to how many times one is contained in the other. That is what division is, and that is what fractions express. Ratio, however, does have a slightly different concept in that it is used as a base from which other similar comparative sizes and quantities can be obtained.

Write a ratio on the paper as 8 : 4. Say something like this: "The ratio 8 : 4 (eight to four) tells us that 8 is twice the size of 4. Any other numbers that show the same relationship are equal ratios. 6 : 3 and 14 : 7 are equal, not in quantity but in *comparison*. When the numbers are divided, the answers will be equal in quantity also. Their ratios have the relationship of two to one.

"Their equality is often expressed as a proportion, rather than by using the equal sign. 8 : 4 :: 6 : 3 means that eight is to four as six is to three.

"If you were to draw two rectangles, one eight inches long and four inches wide, the other six inches long and three inches wide, they would be in *proportion*. Their sizes would be in agreement, harmonious in appearance.

"If you know one ratio and are asked to find another, follow this simple method. 8 : 4 :: 6 : 3. Notice that the two on the outside, called the *extremes*, are 8 and 3. $8 \times 3 = 24$. The product of the other two numbers, called the *means* because they're in the middle, is the same. This can also be written in this way:

$$\frac{8}{4} = \frac{6}{3}$$

The numbers diagonally across from each other show the extremes and the means of the proportion. $8 \times 3 = 24$, $6 \times 4 = 24$.

"If you know the two numbers in one ratio, and one number of the other ratio, set your problem up like this:

$$\frac{8}{4} = \frac{6}{-}$$

Since 6×4 must equal three times the unknown part, then 24 divided by 8 will equal that part. It has to be 3. It won't matter where the missing number is; just multiply the numbers that are diagonally across, and divide by the other number."

Make up some others for the child to solve, for example:

$$\frac{-}{4} : \frac{9}{12}, \qquad 4 \times 9 = 36, \qquad 36 \div 12 = 3$$

If your child has learned how to perform the processes of multiplication with decimals and how to find the "missing numbers" in multiplication and division problems, he should have no trouble with percentage.

Have him look at these:

$$2 \times 3 = 6 \qquad 6 \div 2 = 3 \qquad 6 \div 3 = 2$$

The product, six, is used as the dividend in each case to find either one of the two numbers multiplied.

Similarly,

$$6 \times .02 = .12; \qquad .12 \div 6 = .02; \qquad .12 \div .02 = 6$$

Say something like this: "There are three terms or symbols used in percentage problems:

"1. The *base* is the original or the whole amount.
"2. The *rate* is the per cent, decimal, or fraction.
"3. The *percentage* is a part of the base or original amount."

There are basically three types of problems that beginners in percentage are asked to solve:

    1. Find the percentage.
    2. Find the base.
    3. Find the rate.

Formulas are often given:

$$B \times R = P; \qquad \frac{P}{B} = R; \qquad \frac{P}{R} = B$$

Those are based on the same principle as shown in the problem $2 \times 3 = 6$. *6* represents the percentage and is the number to be divided to find the *2* and *3*. In percentage, the *P*, or percentage, is always the number to be divided to find the rate and base. It is always put above the line in the fraction, always inside the lines in a division problem:

$$B \overline{)P}; \qquad R \overline{)P}$$

Continue: "The rate is the number that is expressed as a decimal. It may have a per cent sign after it; if so, you must take the sign off. You can't use *that* while multiplying or dividing, so drop it and use a decimal instead. Put a decimal point where it will mean hundredths. There must be two places substituted for every per cent sign. $15\% = .15$; $3\% = .03$; $.3\% = .003$. Count the places: there are two more than there were in each case.

"Every decimal has a fraction equivalent; a decimal, expressing hundredths, of course, can be expressed also as a fraction having 100 for a denominator. $\frac{5}{100}$ is the same as .50 or 50%. Many of the fractions can be reduced to lower terms:

$$\frac{50}{100} = \frac{1}{2}."$$

The child will be given a table of equivalents or *aliquot* parts to learn. Aliquot means an exact divisor. When we say that $\frac{1}{4} = 25\%$, we mean that 25 divides 100 into 4 parts.

Continue: "Decimals are all just fractional parts of one whole, the same as fractions. Often it is simpler to use the fractions; sometimes it is easier to use the decimals.

"In solving problems, always look for the base, the percentage, and the rate. The one that isn't given is the one you must find. Once you know that, you'll know what to do. If the base and rate are there, multiply. If the percentage is given, one of the others will be missing and you'll have to divide the percentage by whichever one of those is given. The *base* comes after the word 'of' in many problems. Mark the parts in any problem you are asked to solve."

Write these examples and have the child mark the parts:

$\overset{R\quad B}{\text{Find 8\% of 38}}$ (P?) $30 \times .08 = 2.4$

$\overset{P}{\text{6 is what per cent of 18?}}\overset{B}{}$ (R?) $\frac{6}{18} = \frac{1}{3} = .33\frac{1}{3} = 33\frac{1}{3}\%$

$\overset{P\quad R}{\text{3 is 6\% of what number?}}$ (B?) $\frac{3}{.06} = .06\overline{)3.00}^{\,50}$

The part after the word "of" is the base. The one with the % sign is the rate. The other one is the percentage.

Be sure that the student learns to:

1. Analyze the problem and mark the parts, B, R, and P.
2. Look for which of the three is missing.
3. Decide whether to multiply or divide.
4. Always use the percentage as the dividend.

The words *medium, intermediate, median, mean,* and *average* are all related to the concept of *middle*. In Latin, the word *medius* means middle.

Say something like this to the child: "*Medium* size is between large and small size. *Intermediate* describes a place between two other places or things, not necessarily at the exact middle or center. *Inter* in Latin means *between*. A *median* is a numeral in the middle position of a sequence of numerals that are placed in an order of increasing or decreasing values. No other attention is given to the values or amounts that the numerals represent, only to their position.

"In the number sequence 2, 3, 5, 7, 8, the numeral 5 is the median because it has the same number of numerals on each side.

"What is the median of these: 15, 14, 14, 10, 7? Yes, it is *14*. What is the median in 1, 1, 4, 4, 6, 7, 7, 9? The middle is between *4* and *6*, so the median would be *5*."

Have the child arrange some numbers in increasing or decreasing sequences and find the medians.

Then say: "The word *mene* in Middle English was also taken from the Latin *medius*. Our word *mean*, used here, refers to quantity. A *mean* is the quantity in the middle of a group of quantities.

The Old English word *midd* appears in *middle, midday, midway,* and various other words referring to halfway marks or the center point.

"Average also refers to quantity. *A* in Latin means *to, verus* means *truth.* Average is the true *mean.*

"The sum of 2, 3, 5, 7 and 8 is 25. If each of those numerals named the same amount, what would those five numbers have to be? 25 divided by 5 equals 5. $5 + 5 + 5 + 5 + 5 = 25$. 5 is the average. *First add the numbers to find the sum. To find the average, count the numerals and divide the* sum *by that number.*

"The average is always larger than the smallest number in the group and smaller than the largest."

Chapter 47

MEASUREMENTS

There are two things your child must know if he is to learn how to measure and how to solve problems concerned with measurement: He must learn the names given to definite quantities and amounts, and he must know how many of the smaller ones are contained in each successive larger one. He should understand each concept and be able to retain it.

He must know how to change from one size to another. Memorization is often done by rote.

An easy manner in which to explain the need for such memory training is to say something like: "To measure in any way means to find the size—that is, to find out how much of something we have, how heavy it is, how much space it covers, or how much space it fills. To communicate this information to others, we must have standards that will be understood and recognized by them, as well as by ourselves.

"Governments usually agree on the standards to be used, and these standards are called *tables,* which comes originally from the French *tablette* (or little table), which again comes to us in the word used for packages of writing paper, *tablets.*"

The main tables that the student will be called upon to memorize are:

Liquid measure:

$$2 \text{ cups} = 1 \text{ pint (pt.)}$$
$$2 \text{ pints} = 1 \text{ quart (qt.)}$$
$$4 \text{ quarts} = 1 \text{ gallon (gal.)}$$

Dry measure:

$$2 \text{ pints} = 1 \text{ quart (qt.)}$$
$$8 \text{ quarts} = 1 \text{ peck (pk.)}$$
$$4 \text{ pecks} = 1 \text{ bushel (bu.)}$$

Weight:

$$16 \text{ ounces (oz.)} = 1 \text{ pound (lb.)}$$
$$100 \text{ pounds} = 1 \text{ hundredweight (cwt.)}$$
$$2000 \text{ pounds} = 1 \text{ ton (T.)}$$
$$2240 \text{ pounds} = 1 \text{ long ton}$$

Length or linear measure:

$$12 \text{ inches (in.)} = 1 \text{ foot (ft.)}$$
$$3 \text{ feet} = 1 \text{ yard (yd.)}$$
$$36 \text{ inches } (3 \times 12) = 1 \text{ yard}$$
$$5\tfrac{1}{2} \text{ yards} = 1 \text{ rod (rd.)}$$
$$16\tfrac{1}{2} \text{ feet } (5\tfrac{1}{2} \times 3) = 1 \text{ rod}$$
$$320 \text{ rods} = 1 \text{ mile (mi.)}$$
$$5280 \text{ feet } (320 \times 16\tfrac{1}{2}) = 1 \text{ mile}$$

Square measure:

$$144 \text{ square inches (sq. in.)} = 1 \text{ square foot (sq. ft.)}$$
$$9 \text{ square feet} = 1 \text{ square yard (sq. yd.)}$$
$$160 \text{ square rods} = 1 \text{ acre}$$
$$640 \text{ acres} = 1 \text{ square mile (sq. mi.)}$$

Volume—cubic measure:

$$1728 \text{ cubic inches (cu. in.)} = 1 \text{ cubic foot (cu. ft.)}$$
$$27 \text{ cubic feet (cu. ft.)} = 1 \text{ cubic yard (cu. yd.)}$$

The memory will be helped considerably if the child can visualize and handle amounts and their relative sizes. Aids to this process, which can easily be made into enjoyable games, will be found in most households—foot rules, kitchen scales and weights, kitchen measuring cups, milk containers, food packages, etc.

There is one basic way, also, of teaching the concept of changing quantities with which the learning process can be started.

MATERIALS NEEDED

1. Two boxes or containers, each of which will contain 10 marbles or other small objects.
2. One box or container that will hold 20 similar objects.
3. Paper and pencil.

The child must fully comprehend the idea that the one large container will hold a larger number of objects than one small container, and as many as the two small containers.

Say something like this: "Here are two small boxes. Put ten objects in each box. Are there more or less in two boxes, than there are in only one box? More, of course. How can you find a larger number in arithmetic? Yes, by adding or multiplying. In these problems we shall multiply because it takes less time than adding. $10 \times 2 = 20$. The number of small objects in the containers is always larger than the number of containers.

"Now take the larger box. How many objects will that hold? It will hold the same amount as the two smaller boxes—20. Put the 10 objects in the larger box. How many of the smaller boxes can you fill with 20 objects? Will the number of boxes be more or less than 10? It will be less, of course. To make a number smaller, we can subtract or divide. In this case, we will use the opposite of multiplication, division. 20 divided by 2. We need two of the smaller containers to hold 20 objects."

This activity may be continued with more containers and more objects, if necessary. Be sure that the child has the idea of multiplying to find the number of objects and dividing to find the number of containers.

Most of the confusion with measurements results from the child's multiplying to find something smaller and dividing to find something larger. He must realize that it is the *number* of things he is finding, not the things themselves.

Chapter 48

TIME

Time is another way of measuring length. The Old English word *tima* was related to the Icelandic word *timi,* for tide. A tide is a movement of the water of the oceans, which rises and falls at periods close to 12 hours. It was natural that the ancient peoples should associate the length of a day with the tides.

Measurement of time is closely related to the rotation and revolution of the earth, so it is natural to think of it as also going around in the form of a circle. The child will probably think of time doing this, since the hands of a clock go around.

Have the child look at this table for time.

60 seconds = 1 minute	7 days = 1 week	
60 minutes = 1 hour	(30 days) 4 weeks = 1 month	
24 hours = 1 day	12 months = 1 year	
	365 days = 1 year	

Say something like this: "To understand time, we can start with the *day.* The earth turns on its axis once a day." (You could turn

235

a ball around once to show what this means.) "We face toward the sun for half of this time, 12 hours, and away from it for the other half. That's 24 hours for one time around. It goes around like that about 365 times while going on a path all the way around the sun once." (You could demonstrate this path by taking the ball around some object representing the sun, in an elliptical pattern.)

"During this time, most of the earth has four *seasons*. The word *season* is taken from the Latin word *satio*, meaning *a time of planting*. The planting and harvesting of grain and fruit is governed by the seasons—the time of the year. *Spring*, from the Old English word *springan*, meaning to *jump* or *leap*, is the name of the season when plants spring from the earth. *Summer*, from the Old English *sumor*, which indicated a time when plants had their period of development or growth, is the warmest season, the time when plants grow. *Autumn*, from the Latin word *autumnus*, which refers to *passing down to a decline* (or *fall*, which also indicates a downward movement) is the period of year when plants are beginning to mature and die; the fruit and grain ripen and are ready for harvest. The word *fall*, as the name of the season, is generally used in the United States. *Winter*, the last season of the year, is the same word that was used in Old English to describe the period of finality—the end of things.

"During the 365 days that make up a year, the moon appears and disappears from sight twelve times. These periods are called *months*; primitive peoples called them *moons*. Some months have more than 30 days."

Perhaps the best way for a child to remember the number of days in each month, is for him to learn some version of the old rhyme:

> Thirty days have September,
> April, June, and November;
> All the rest have thirty-one,
> Save February, which alone
> Has twenty-eight, and one day more
> We add to it, one year in four.

He usually remembers the number of days in February, especially when he understands the significance of *leap year*, which was put into our calendar as a means of equalizing the length of the ordinary year and the astronomical year. He should know that leap years are those that are divisible by four; the entire number must be divided. (Century years, such as 1900, have to be divisible by 400, instead of by four.)

If the child knows the number of days in February, he can remember the number sequence, 4-6-9-11. Those are the numbers of the months that have 30 days; all of the others, of course, have 31.

The names of the months are interesting, and their derivations usually appeal to children.

Say something like this: "*Janus* was the name of a Roman god with two faces. January, because it faces the old year and the new, was given his name. February received its name from the Roman Festival of the Purification, called *februa*, which was celebrated at that time of year. March was named for the Roman god of war, *Mars*; April, for the Latin *Aprilis*; May, for the Old English *Maius*, a time to gather flowers; June, for *Juno*, a Roman goddess. The old Roman calendar went on from there to the seventh, eighth, ninth, and tenth months, all having names including the Roman numbers—September, October, November, and December. When Julius Caesar was in power, he added a month, July, to commemorate his birthday; not to be outdone, Augustus Caesar later added August."

The names of the months are not too difficult to spell, if the child learns them in parts. For instance, make three short lines, for January. ___ ___ ___. Have him write *Jan* on the first line, *u* on the next and *ary* on the last. If he becomes used to putting the *ru* together in February, the rest is easy. If he does have trouble, let him trace the shapes of the letters with his finger as he says their names.

A month is divided into approximately four weeks. Explain that a few extra days must be added to make the year of 365 days.

Continue: "In the Bible, we are told that God made the world in six days and rested on the seventh. The first day is named Sunday, for the sun; Monday is named for the moon; Tuesday, in Old English, was called *Tiwesdaeg*, which was a translation of *Martis dies*, the Latin for *day of Mars*. Wednesday and Thursday were named for the Scandinavian gods *Woden* and *Thor*; Friday for a Norse goddess, *Frigg*; Saturday, for the Roman god *Saturn*."

If the child is interested in these names, he may want to find further information; encourage him to make use of books at home or in the library for research.

The months of the year, the weeks, and the days are shown on calendars. *Calend,* in Old English, meant the *beginning of a month;* calendars usually have pages beginning with the first of each month.

The remainder of the divisions of time are shown with clocks or watches. Have your child look up information about sundials and hourglasses and see how they were used before clocks.

The Middle English word for an instrument to measure time was *clokke,* from the Old English word for bell, *clugge.*

For convenience in measuring time, an hour is divided into 60 smaller parts, called minutes. The Latin *minutus* means *a small part.* An hour is divided a second time into still smaller parts. These are called *seconds,* for the ordinal numeral related to *two.*

If your child cannot tell time, here is an activity that may help him. If you like, you could make copies of the figures shown on a piece of paper.

Say something like this: "Look at the large circle. It represents an hour; the first small circle represents a minute, and the second, smaller circle represents a second.

"Now, think of the large circle turning around, quite slowly, once. Think of the minute circle turning faster, going around 60 times while the hour-circle is turning only once. The second small circle is spinning very fast, going around 3600 times during the same time. That will give you an idea of the relative speeds with which hours, minutes, and seconds pass by.

"Circles, such as these, would not be good for telling time; they would be confusing to us, especially if we had to keep track of how many times each turned. A clock is made with only one circle, with arrows or 'hands' that point to the hours and minutes that have passed. The hour hand is the shortest one; you can remember that because the word *hour* is shorter than the word *minute.* The shorter word goes with the shorter hand; the longer word goes with the longer hand.

"Think of the three circles, and the hands of the clock, working together. As the hour-circle turns once, the hour hand moves slowly from one number to the other, say from 1 to 2. When the hour hand is pointing *directly* at the numeral 1, it is exactly one o'clock. When it is between the *1* and the *2*, it is some time before two o'clock.

"The number of minutes before, and after, is shown by the minute hand. While the minute-circle turns around five times, the minute hand moves from one numeral to the next. Starting at *12*, it takes five minutes to move to the numeral *1*, another five minutes to move to the numeral 2, and so on. You can count by fives. When the minute hand points to *1*, say five, when it points to *2*, say ten, when it points to *3*, say fifteen. Go right on: 20, 25, 30. When the minute-hand is at *6*, that's halfway, so we call it half-past; then we usually begin to say it's so many minutes before the next hour. That's only fair. 25 minutes to two, 20 minutes to two, 15 minutes to two, and all the way around to twelve. Then it's the next hour, and the hour hand will have arrived at the next numeral.

"What time is it, by the clock in the illustration? The hour hand is a little bit past *1*, so it's sometime near one o'clock; the minute hand is at *3*. Begin counting at the *12*, by fives: 5, 10, 15 minutes after one."

Have the child practice telling time; help him to establish the position of the hour hand, then the minute hand.

Explain that second hands are not shown on clocks and watches unless there is some need, as on stop watches used for timing events where seconds are important.

Chapter 49

MONEY

Learning the table for money seldom causes a child any trouble.

He might like to know that *cent,* from the Latin word *centum,* is one-hundredth of a dollar; that the name *penny* is from the Old English word *pening,* which was a coin of varying value. The plural of penny, *pence,* was used for other coins, such as *twopence, fourpence,* and so on. The word *penny* is also used to describe the size of nails; at one time, if a nail cost fourpence, it was called a fourpenny nail! Now, the names penny and cent are given to the same coin, usually made of copper. Pennies used to be called *coppers,* too.

A *nickel* is so called because of the metal of which it is, in part, made. The word *dime,* from the Latin *decima,* meaning one-tenth, is given to our silver coin worth one-tenth of a dollar. The name *dollar* comes from *dalar* and *thaller,* names of ancient coins first made in a valley in Germany. *Thal* is a German word for valley.

A *quarter,* of course, is a fourth or quarter of a dollar; the name applied to a *half-dollar* is obvious. The weight of the coins is in proportion to the weight of the silver dollar. There are gold dollars also, although they are not in use. Paper dollars are generally used.

Your child might find it interesting to do some research on *bills* and find out what amounts of money are represented by paper in our country and whose picture appears on each.

To help your child learn the values of coins, use play money or round pieces of paper cut the size of coins and marked with their values.

Have him "balance" amounts in piles—100 pennies, 20 nickels, ten dimes, four quarters, two half-dollars, and one dollar. Do the same with other amounts—two dimes and a nickel on one side, a quarter on the other; or five pennies and a nickel balancing a dime.

This should help him to learn how to make change.

Since our system of money is based on decimals, you can use the instructions given under decimals to show your child how to keep the decimal points in line for adding and subtraction and, when necessary, how to handle the decimals in division and multiplication.

Say something like this: "The *cents* in a sum of money show a fractional part of one dollar. To change dollars to cents, multiply the number of dollars by 100—the answer must be larger; to change cents to dollars, divide the number of cents by 100 (point off two decimal places)—the number of dollars must be smaller." Give him some examples for practice.

Have your child practice making the signs used for money.

Say something like this: "The dollar sign is placed *before* the number of dollars. The cent sign is placed after the number of cents; it is used only for amounts less than one dollar, and *never* if the decimal point and dollar sign is used. $\frac{15}{100}$ of a dollar is shown by writing $ .15. To use the ¢ sign would be to repeat the name of cents. 15¢ is proper, however.

The dollar sign is said to go back to the pirates' "pieces of eight," which were Spanish dollars equal to 8 *reals*. It is a broken 8, and the lines represent two pillars of Hercules.

SUMMATION:
PREPARING FOR
LIFELONG LEARNING

As American citizens, we are very conscious of the responsibility our Constitution has bestowed upon us. We accept without reservation the tenet that all men are created equal.

We hold this belief especially sacred in respect to education.

Education—free and equal education—is the prerogative of every one of us. Our conviction that knowledge is the basic answer to our problems grows increasingly stronger. Thus, any criticism of an educational theory that we believe to be valid sends us automatically to arms. But while we may disagree on where, when, and how education is to be administered, we are one when it comes to the right of every citizen to receive it.

It is easy to find fault and take sides on national issues that encompass divergent opinions. Education is such an issue. Everyone who speaks out about it is trying to encourage acceptance of his own ideas, his own creative thoughts on the subject. Essentially, all that any critic really wants is to hold fast to that truly American right of education for everyone—a type of education that fits the needs of each individual.

Fulfillment of this obligation requires an over-all plan. Equality of rights and similarity of needs are not necessarily synonymous.

A blueprint for education should be so broad in its implications that it embraces the essence of all learning and so inclusive that it permeates a human life from the cradle to the grave. It is of such import that every citizen who has participated should feel that he has played his part in creating a better community, a better state, a better country, and consequently, a better world for posterity.

The over-all plan that has been suggested here is to use all possible means to develop an effective learning process for each individual. Some children may require something more than perception training. If so, they have the right to be checked and cared for physically, emotionally, and physiologically.

Thorough physical education is vital to muscle coordination and to the best possible strength and health of the body. An emotional climate conducive to learning is of equal importance.

The over-all plan should start as early in a child's life as possible. It is composed of simple sequential blocks of training, which are in themselves based on truths. There can be no controversy about the presentation. The problem does not concern the techniques of training; it concerns the recognition of the need for such training. The plan itself is so simple that it is deceiving. But look deep and check each step against your own experiences in learning. You may find that some of your own early childhood uncertainties are represented and made clear.

The whole of such an approach can be covered by basic communication patterns. *Communication* here refers to the oral, pictured, and written symbols that represent the abstract ideas that are the basis of all numerals and words. It means, too, both sending and receiving the message.

Such a program hangs on the bare skeleton of messages received through the sensory channels. They speed directly to the brain in various combinations, are united there with each other and associated with many others that have been previously received. But this is not the end. A recognition of the myriad messages must occur if they are to be sorted, recalled, and used to the best advantage without confusion or waste.

It is easy to see, then, how important the training of the sensory channels is, even before we consider what must be recognized, sorted, and stored for recall and communication.

The pertinence and suitability of the messages vary and overlap; as sets containing similar elements, they have some things in common. There are similarities and differences, degrees and sequences of position, shape, size, and so on, that can be perceived by more than one sense. The process of learning can be accelerated by scanning for patterns that can be recognized as basic. Speed and accuracy can be acquired with minimum effort and time for an immediate purpose by using only the stimuli that are needed for clear perception at the moment.

The recognition of these patterns becomes an automatic awareness. What is the magic formula that enables an individual to have this skill of "awareness?" In part, it is one of nature's gifts—but one not always completely cultivated. The most aware person can become more so by the simple, systematic training of each sensory channel to the brain; training will make certain that messages are received and, in turn, communicated to others; training will make use of the eye-ear-hand channels as the core agencies but will not neglect the channels of taste and smell, since these have such great power to assist by association and by subtle adding to the skill of recall.

Special care must be given to the teaming up of the channels. Emphasis should be placed on eye-hand, ear-hand, and eventually, on eye-ear-hand teamwork. Then should come the equally simple sequential training of those channels to perceive similarities and differences, degrees, and sequences in all areas concerned with three-dimensional figures—in their position, direction, and number. This should be followed by the same steps with two-dimensional figures.

Much can and should be done to see that the beginning learner has additional experiences with these concepts in his immediate environment. When he understands the patterns that he perceives, recognizes, and can recall, it is time to widen his horizons with experiences in which he can apply his skills.

Home, school, and community life in general supply these lessons over and over again, for it is of these concepts and their various abstractions that our world is built.

When you are sure that the child knows all the conceivable concepts that have been presented in perception training, and their relationships to each other and to him, it is time to move into abstractions. This move will be easy if he has had the right groundwork.

It is ridiculous for anyone to suppose that any one way of learning is the only way. It is only common sense to find as many ways and patterns as possible, so in any circumstances any particular type of student will have various ways of learning from which to select the one best suited to him.

It would be presumptuous, for example, to say that any one way to learn to read is the only way. Certainly, the teaching of reading should include all the logical ways to attack words, plus all the ways to insure that the student anticipates, understands, and recalls what he has read. The patterns so necessary to good reading must be established in one way or another, and if the child has the perception that gives him the skill to recognize symbols and the things for which they stand, he can soon put aside the "mechanics" and concentrate on the meaning.

Comparison of shapes, recognition of degrees of size, and awareness of the similarities and differences in all the concepts included in perception training result in a logical pattern of thought that is helpful in making solid, rational judgments. This manner of thinking helps in finding a "golden mean"—a happy medium between the extremes that are too often reached by irrational and subjective opinions.

The ability to identify a sphere by its roundness and a cube by its sharp edges without being confused by cones and cylinders, which have some of each, can lead to the proper choice between what is right or wrong, what is important and not important. The same perception that enables a child to scan for sequential patterns can cause him to anticipate reasonable results of certain actions or events, as well as what letter or word or number to expect next. The skill that allows a child to choose the correct symbols to express an idea, whether they be letters, words, or numbers, should bring about a realization that the essence of all things is represented by symbols.

The symbols themselves are not the reality. The familiar quotation, "A rose by any other name would smell as sweet," expresses that very thought. A name is merely a tool to be used for communication—a tool that cannot be ignored if ideas are to be interchanged.

If a child visits a museum, he should not see the things displayed merely as isolated objects. The objects have been selected as symbols of some part of his world. The significance of their relationship to his life, and to the life of others, is the important thing.

As a rule, teachers prepare their classes for these experiences by establishing those relationships before taking field trips. Parents can do the same by relating what is seen to its purpose, use, or reason for being. Nothing is thus isolated from its natural surroundings or its relationships and interrelationships any more than one person is completely separated from any of his fellow men. What a person does and how he acts has an effect on all others; a child can learn this by being conscious of relationships, sequential patterns, causes, and results.

A symbol is a shape with size, and sometimes with a specific color or texture. It has a definite purpose, and it is different from other symbols. It is expressed at times by sound or motion. It has a relationship with something else and its position is important to show that relationship. A child may know what the symbol stands for before he learns the symbol itself. He must learn to put them together in order to live in today's world.

For example, he must learn to obey signs and lights at street corners; he must know the meaning of the bell that tells him that class is over; he must learn the letters used to make words, the words used to express ideas, and the numerals that enable him to count, to express the relationship between numbers, and to compute amounts.

Most children have the intelligence to learn these things. The intelligence may, however, remain hidden unless they have been given an opportunity to use all their senses, all their potential to learn.

If a child does not respond at home or in school, usually it is *not* because he has no ability to learn. It may be because he has not been shown how to organize his thoughts, how to put them in an orderly sequential pattern or how to use the proper symbols to express them.

This is the reason for helping him to perceive not only with his auditory and visual senses, but with all outer and inner senses that will make his reception of stimuli complete enough for him to respond fully and adequately.

A child who has acquired an inner feeling of position and gone on from there to learn direction of movement has gained a very useful sense of orientation. He can learn the relation of north and south, east and west, by the sun and moon and often by familiar landmarks. A child with a sureness of position usually has little trouble with maps and knows where he is in relation to other parts of his state, country, and the world.

He should be able to orient himself in history as well. His place in a time-line of the ages is important to his understanding of the subject. If he has a sequential sense of what has come before and can imagine what might come in the future, his comprehension is more acute.

Grammar, arithmetic, the sciences and arts, literature, reading, spelling—each of these is an accumulation and result of what has gone before. One thing follows another in orderly, related, sequential patterns, and on that premise a simple plan of teaching can be formed.

When the child has acquired this foundation, then and only then will he be able to fulfill his destiny. He can then show the world what is in his mind.

Creativity may be his own particular response to the stimuli he has received through any or all of his senses. He will not be limited to any one area. Whether his special interest turns out to be science, art, or human relations, his success will be greater because it is the result of more than a single skill. The cabling of one-skill with all the others will make it possible for him to put into his work or hobby more of himself, and beyond this, it will be beneficial to others. He will be able to communicate not with an isolated few, but with the vast majority of his fellow humans.

The more fundamental skills the child has mastered, the closer he is to discovering the common elements in the minds of all people and reducing them to the common denominator of understanding. If this can encompass the learning of many languages, including the nuances of his own, the child can project his usefulness still further.

The comprehension of relationships and number sequences is not confined to mathematics. The ability to recognize them can be applied to all fields of endeavor. A child must have this skill to become a good mechanical reader, just as he needs the ability to abstract meaning to become an intelligent reader.

If a child serves his apprenticeship by learning the fundamental skills and the vocabulary that goes with them, he is ready to enter any competition with which he is faced. It is not fair to place him into any competition until he has had a chance to develop and use every one of his senses and has been given many different ways of learning from which he can choose his own.

He must be able to feel adequate and successful in as many ways as possible, so he has the desire and even the compulsion to try more and more things, doing his utmost in each. The fact that someone else does better in any one particular area need not cause him to feel frustration and discouragement.

A parent may not realize that a child has untapped resources that need only be released. Every human being has these resources, and probably no one has ever used them all. Even perception training will not make everyone a genius, but it cannot help but raise the aptitude of every recipient to greater heights.

It has been said that a creative person is one who is able to register and avail himself of a greater number of experiences than one who is not creative. It is reasonable to suppose that perception training would bring out a greater degree of creativity in any child.

Fluency, an ability to communicate with ease, is another sign of creativity. To perceive, to scan, to sort and choose, to use and produce with accuracy and speed is the purpose of perception training. Creativity, as such, cannot be forced. But if it is there, it will be made evident.

For example, your child might be asked to interpret a passage he has read. Remind him that his senses will help him. What was seen or heard? Was anything smelled or tasted? What reactions came through each sense, and what relationship could be perceived? What was the sequence in time and occurrence—the cause and result of each idea or event? Often, children who have been classified as unimaginative or uncreative can be given confidence in this manner and can be started on the road to fluency.

There are many sources of education in a community as well as at home. A child can perform helpful tasks around the house and yard, using and supplementing his training. A sense of responsibility and relationships can add order and beauty to his life, whether they be concerned with his own appearance or with that of his surroundings. Shape, size, texture, color—all these things to which he can become sensitive are vitally important. If you take your child to the stores or markets, he will have an opportunity to advance his knowledge of numbers, amounts, and values. He can help make selections and have practice in comparison, judgment, and logical choice.

Remember that he is always learning and often may have to defer to someone else's judgment. If he makes an error, he probably can recognize it as such and improve upon it the next time.

It is a mistake to allow a child to assume grown-up responsibility too early. He needs the assurance that in the areas he has not mastered, he has someone to look up to and depend upon.

Visits to libraries, museums, civic organizations, police and fire stations, and industrial plants are of great value in showing a child what is done for him and his community and how it is done. Trips around the country broaden his knowledge, give him many opportunities to add to his collections, and deepen his sense of geography and history. If trips are not possible, there are government bureaus, travel agencies, and industries to which he can write for pictures and folders. All this will add to the sum total of experience that will make his learning full and complete.

Since the purpose of education is to fit a child for his life and for the world of which he is an indivisible part, it is never too early for him to begin to utilize what his world has to offer him.

It is important that he feel an integral part of his family, his community, and his country; that he know his responsibility to them and be proud and appreciative of what they have given and will give to him.

The symbols that stand for mother, father, school, teacher, church, and government, should remain as untarnished as possible. Perhaps some things about reality are occasionally not admirable, but reality cannot be denied. A child should know all he can about the ideal for which the symbols stand and recognize what is good—and what is bad—about the reality. He must know that when he makes mistakes, others have made them too. But he must have a sound basis for making an evaluation so he will not accept fallacies as truths. He must know that perfection is something for which everyone should strive, but something that can be reached only by trying and failing, and then by trying and trying again.

It is an exciting world that each one of us lives in. Add a family to it, and suddenly it takes on dynamic dimensions. Every shared experience becomes filled with meaning, and as we establish patterns for our children we find—perhaps sheepishly—new vistas for ourselves.

Sensory training, as it concerns perception and patterns of learning, suddenly opens up exciting treasure chests that add to our own delights as well as supplement the educational heritage that belongs to our sons and daughters, and to every boy and girl in the modern world.

APPENDIX

The average sixth-grade-level child should be able to use and understand most of the words in the lists comprising this appendix.

Preschool children will be able to start with the simplest words and then increase their vocabularies gradually, according to individual ability and the opportunities they have to hear and use new words.

After the student has started school, you should continue to encourage him to use more and more of these and other words, as he progresses to higher grades.

A good dictionary or thesaurus will be invaluable in finding more synonyms (words of similar meaning) and antonyms (words of opposite meaning). A good reference source of this type will encourage your child to discover for himself various nuances and shades of meaning in words he uses regularly or occasionally.

Words to Describe Movement, Position, Direction and Time

Likes and Differences

start   stop
begin   end
first   last
give   take
give   receive
don   doff
put on   take off
beginning   conclusion
here   there
near   far

Degrees and Sequences

near   nearer   nearest
far   farther   farthest
high   higher   highest
first   middle   last
first   between   last
top   between   bottom
beginning   center   end
near   medium   far
close   medium   distant
first   second   third

253

Likes and Differences

close   distant
tight   loose
left   right
east   west
north   south
this side   that side
this way   that way
in   out
into   out of
center   edge
inside   outside
include   exclude
open   close
free   enclosed
up   down
over   under
above   below
top   bottom
head   foot
high   low
lift   drop
raise   lower
vertex   base
zenith   nadir
ceiling   floor
sky   earth
tip   toe
now   then
past   future
before   after
early   late
immediately   any time
temporary   permanent
awhile   always
never   forever
finite   infinite

Degrees and Sequences

past   present   future
never   sometimes   always
early   on time   late

WORDS TO DESCRIBE SOUND

Likes and Differences	*Degrees and Sequences*
silence noise	loud louder loudest
low high	low lower lowest
soft shrill	soft softer softest
faint loud	shrill shriller shrillest
sweet harsh	sweet sweeter sweetest
silence sound	harsh harsher harshest
whisper shout	clear clearer clearest
clear hoarse	hoarse hoarser hoarsest
gentle raucous	high higher highest
harmony discord	soft medium shrill
high deep	low medium loud
cheerful somber	low medium high
rhythmic nonrhythmic	
high-pitched low-pitched	

WORDS TO DESCRIBE COLOR

Likes and Differences	*Degrees and Sequences*
light dark	light lighter lightest
black white	dark darker darkest
bright dull	clear clearer clearest
soft glaring	light medium dark
pleasing displeasing	primary secondary comple-
pleasant unpleasant	mentary
harmonious clashing	
pure mixed	
clear shaded	
primary complementary	

WORDS TO DESCRIBE TEXTURE

Likes and Differences

soft   hard
smooth   rough
fine   coarse
tight   loose
pleasing   displeasing
flat   grained

Degrees and Sequences

soft   softer   softest
hard   harder   hardest
smooth   smoother   smoothest
fine   finer   finest
coarse   coarser   coarsest
flat   flatter   flattest
soft   medium   hard
smooth   medium   rough
rough   rougher   roughest

WORDS TO DESCRIBE TASTE AND ODOR

Likes and Differences

sweet   acid
sweet   sour
sweet   bitter
mild   sharp
mild   hot
pleasant   unpleasant
agreeable   disagreeable
tasty   distasteful
good   bad
bland   spicy
bland   flavorful
pleasant   putrid
fresh   rancid

Degrees and Sequences

acid   more acid   most acid
sweet   sweeter   sweetest
sour   sourer   sourest
mild   milder   mildest
sharp   sharper   sharpest
hot   hotter   hottest
good   better   best
bad   worse   worst
spicy   spicier   spiciest
bland   more bland   most bland
fresh   fresher   freshest
pleasant   more pleasant
                    most pleasant
sweet   medium   sour
good   medium   bad
mild   medium   sharp

Words to Describe Temperature

Likes and Differences	*Degrees and Sequences*
hot cold	hot hotter hottest
warm cool	cold colder coldest
lukewarm coolish	warm warmer warmest
boiling freezing	cool cooler coolest
fire ice	hot medium cold
	hot tepid cool cold

Words to Describe Shape, Size, Weight and Amount

Likes and Differences	*Degrees and Sequences*
big little	big bigger biggest
large small	less lesser least
more less	large larger largest
much little	small smaller smallest
few many	few fewer fewest
some all	thin thinner thinnest
none all	fat fatter fattest
increase decrease	thick thicker thickest
add to take away	narrow narrower narrowest
add subtract	wide wider widest
multiply divide	light lighter lightest
thin fat	heavy heavier heaviest
slender broad	delicate more delicate
thin thick	most delicate
narrow wide	dainty daintier daintiest
light heavy	coarse coarser coarsest
underweight overweight	some more most
delicate heavy	little medium big
dainty coarse	small middle-sized large
force resistance	circle oval rectangle square
	one two three (etc.)
	light medium heavy

INDEX

INDEX

ABOUT THE AUTHORS

Marie Avery's educational career shows a psychological orientation. She has taught widely on elementary and high school levels and holds B.E. and M.A. degrees from the University of California. Mrs. Avery pioneered as a woman in executive work in women's Federal prisons. At present she is serving as an expert in remedial reading, and tutoring in schools in Southern California.

Alice Higgins received her training in education at De Kalb (Illinois) Teachers College and De Paul University. She has Ph.B. and Ed.M. degrees from the latter. As a teacher and principal in the Illinois public school system she gained broad classroom experience on elementary and junior high school levels. Currently an associate in the Coordination Research Corporation at San Marino, California, her educational activity is concentrated in the field of sensory perception and training.